STRINGSTASTIC
GRADE 3

Suitable for any music examination board

By Lorraine Chai

P.O. Box 815, Epping NSW 1710 Australia
www.stringstastic.com
Copyright © 2022 Lorraine Chai

All rights reserved.
Reproduction in whole or in parts for any use whatsoever is strictly prohibited.

THE AUTHOR

Lorraine Chai

Lorraine is a multi-talented instrumentalist, mentor, and international educator. She graduated from the Sydney Conservatorium of Music with a Bachelor of Music Studies in 2008 and completed her Graduate Diploma of Education at the Australian Catholic University a year later.

Having grown up with a musical family, Lorraine began piano lessons at the age of four and violin at the age of six, giving her first violin performance at just seven years of age. Lorraine started teaching violin at the age of 14 and founded a string ensemble at her local church. From there, teaching and performing became her passion.

Lorraine loves finding new and exciting ways students can learn their instruments in a classroom setting as well as in private lessons. Along her musical journey and exposure to the various educational methods including Kodaly, Suzuki, Orff, and Dalcroze, Lorraine has also attended Alexander Technique workshops and has found that she can integrate these various methods into her own teaching technique for the benefit of her students.

Lorraine has extensive ensemble and orchestral experience in Malaysia and in Australia. Lorraine is currently the Music Director of Stringstastic Pty Ltd. She also co-ordinates instrumental programs and runs string ensembles for some of Sydney's most celebrated schools.

PREFACE

Stringstastic Grade 3 follows on from the knowledge gained in Grade 2 and is specifically suited for violinists of all ages who are quick learners or who are interested in successfully completing music theory exams.

Every time you see these icons, these are what they mean

 - NOTE/REMINDER

 - PLAY on your instrument

For extra resources, go to www.stringstastic.com to download them for free.

Have fun!!

ACKNOWLEDGEMENT

This book was made possible with the encouragement of family and friends.
I would like to thank the following for their advice and input in making this book possible.

Dr. Rita Crews OAM, FMusA (honoris causa), PhD(UNE), BA(Hons), AMusTCL, GradCertDistEd (UNE), FMusicolASMC, HonFNMSM, DipMus (honoris causa) (AICM) MIMT, MACE, MMTA, JP.

Mary Nemet AMusA, is a prominent string educator, AMEB Examiner, Reviews Editor for AUSTA Stringendo and contributor to Strings USA

CONTENTS

4	Revision
8	Alto Clef
11	Time Signature
12	Duplets and Triplets
15	Anacrusis
17	Creating a Rhythm to a Given Couplet
20	Key Signature
25	Scale Degrees
28	Tiny Revision
30	Intervals and their Quality
32	Dominant Triads
36	Primary Triads
38	Chord Progression
39	2nd Inversion
41	Writing a Bass Line
43	Composition
45	Real and Tonal Sequences
46	4-Part Vocal Style
49	Cadences
52	Revision
54	Transposition
58	Similar Motion vs. Contrary Motion
60	Musical Words and Symbols
63	Final Revision
66	Analysis

Graded theory sample papers from different examination boards can be found on www.stringstastic.com.

Revision

1. **Name the notes.** (Use capital letters.)

2. **Tick the correct definition of the words below.**

   A. An ostinato is a ......
   - ◯ repeated balancing act
   - ◯ repeated rhythmic and pitch pattern that moves up or down by one note each time
   - ◯ repeated rhythmic and pitch pattern

   B. Sequence is a ......
   - ◯ repeated balancing act
   - ◯ repeated rhythmic and pitch pattern that moves up or down by one note each time
   - ◯ repeated rhythmic and pitch pattern

3. Name these intervals by number and quality.

perfect 4th

4. Cross out the incorrect answers.

leggiero	lightly	sm~~oothly~~
Vivace	fast and lively	viper
grazioso	gorilla	gracefully
A minor	has ONE sharp	has no sharps or flats
slur	notes are the same letter names and held the entire value	notes are different letter names and played smoothly

5. Below are different kinds of possible rhythm. Circle those showing syncopated rhythm.

  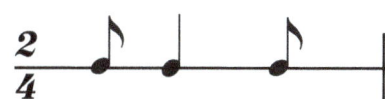

6. What is the relative major scale for E minor? _____

7. What is the relative minor scale for C major? _____

8. Which scale has TWO sharps in its key signature? _____

9. Which scale has THREE flats in its key signature? _____

5

10. Write a 4 bar rhythm using the note and rest values which you have learnt. Include at least THREE rests in every rhythm.

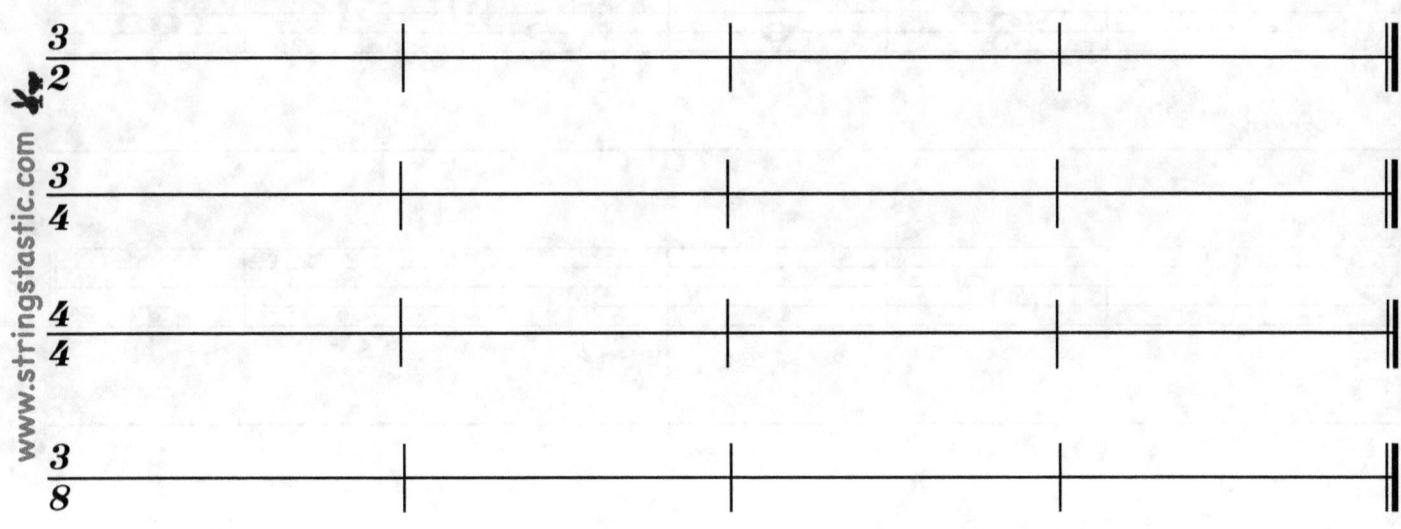

11. Write a tune using notes of the tonic triad of D major to these given rhythms below.

12. Fill in the boxes with correctly grouped rests to complete the bars.

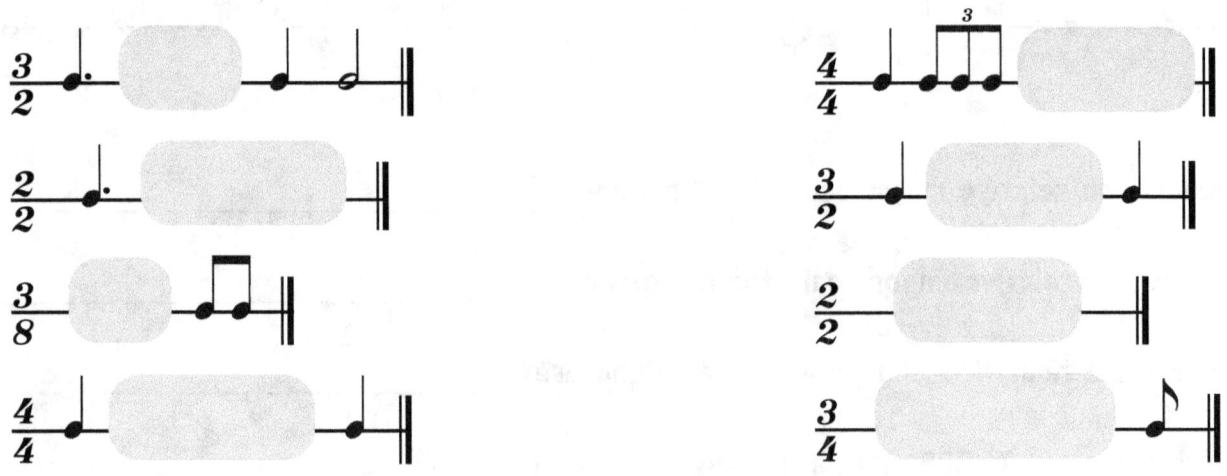

13. **Write out these scales and arpeggios accordingly.**

E harmonic minor
- Draw a treble clef
- Use key signature
- One octave descending only
- Use crotchet notes
- Complete the scale with a double bar line

A melodic minor
- Draw a bass clef
- Use accidentals
- One octave in an ascending and descending order
- Use minim notes
- Complete the scale with a double bar line

D major arpeggio
- Draw a treble clef
- Use accidentals
- One octave in an ascending and descending order
- Use semibreve notes
- Complete the scale with a double bar line

B minor arpeggio
- Draw a bass clef
- Use key signature
- One octave in a descending and ascending order
- Use quaver notes in pairs
- Complete the scale with a double bar line

Alto Clef

Music written for the viola uses the Alto Clef.

The alto clef looks like numbers on the stave.

In print the alto clef has one thick and one thin line. However we do not need to draw them as printed. Just remember that it looks like these three numbers – 113.

𝄡

The alto clef determines where the C note is located through the use of the TWO curves.

1. Trace these alto clefs and draw a few more of your own.

 The 2 curves meet up on the middle line.

Below are the names of the open string for the viola.
 The cello also has the same open strings as the viola.

(Open strings = name of each string without placing any fingers on it.)

C Cute   **G** Girl   **D** Dances   **A** Around

Below shows where the open strings will be on the alto clef for a violist.

Below is how you would remember the name of the notes on the alto clef.

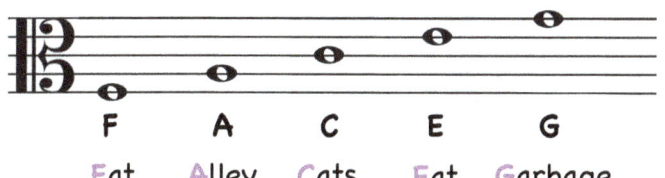

F   A   C   E   G
Fat Alley Cats Eat Garbage

As for the notes in the spaces, all we need to do is use the alphabet which we already know and count up and down between the lines.

 You can make your own acronyms to remember the note names.

2. **Let us see if you can figure out the notes in between.**

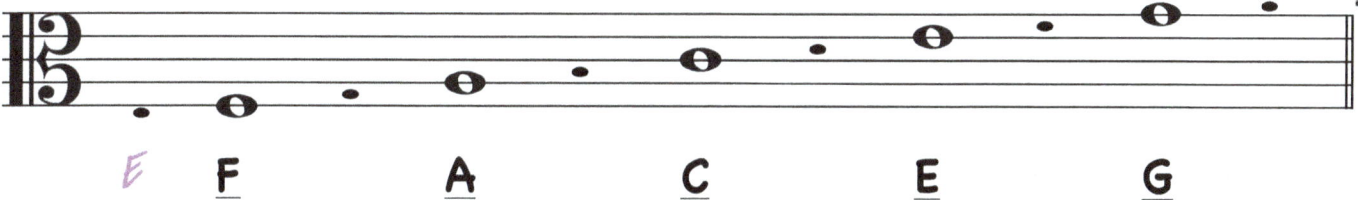

E   F   A   C   E   G

3. **Name these notes.** (Use capital letters.)

4. **Using semibreve notes, draw these notes on the alto clef.**

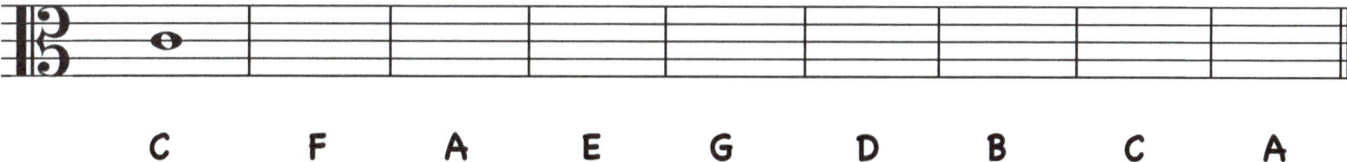

C   F   A   E   G   D   B   C   A

For the curious mind or for those that are thinking of learning the viola, below are the comparisons with the violin on what the notes are on the fingerboard in 1st position.

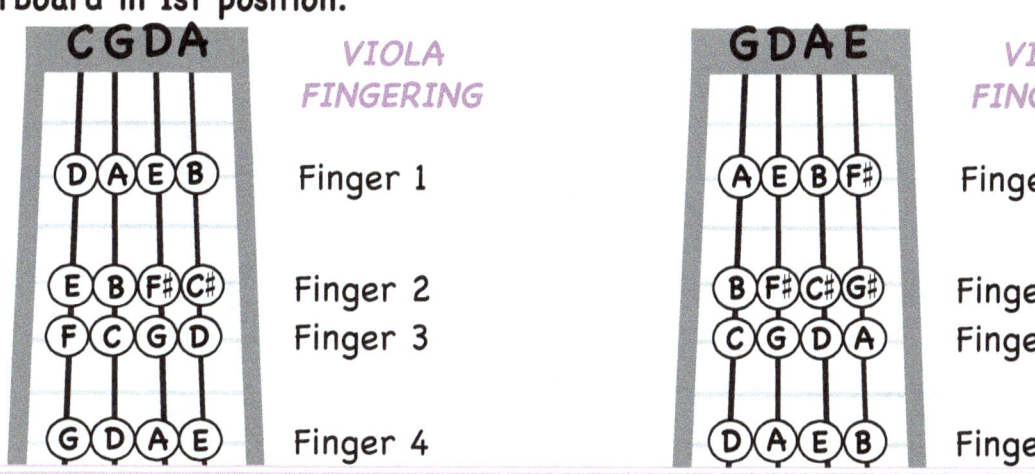

Below is what you call each string player according to the instrument they play.

Violin - violinist

Viola - violist

Cello - cellist

Bass - bassist

(Piano - pianist)

This is what a middle C looks like on all 3 clefs.

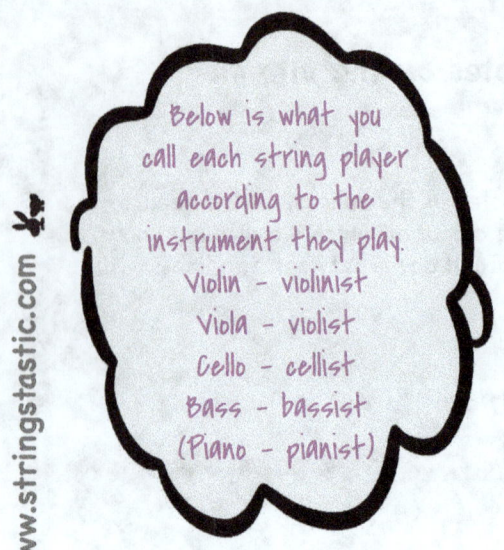

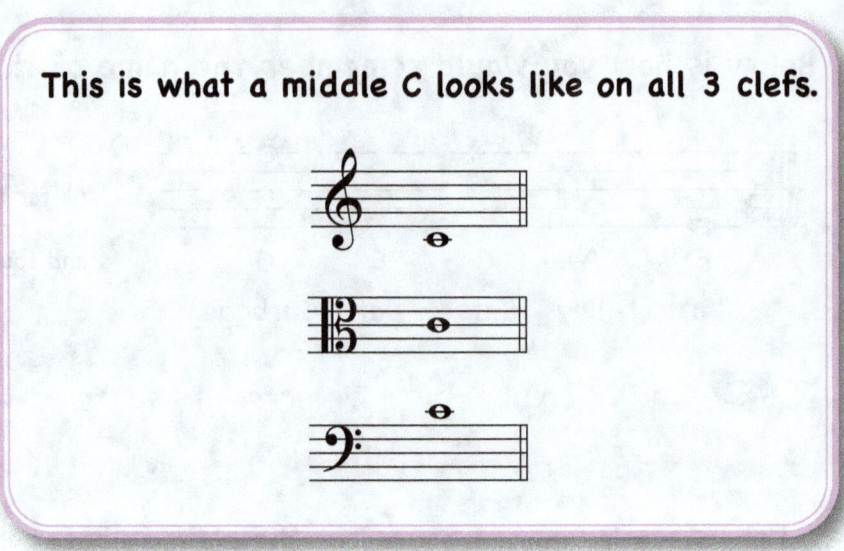

5. Match the letter names to the appropriate notes. (Careful of the clefs.)

A

B

C

D

E

F

G

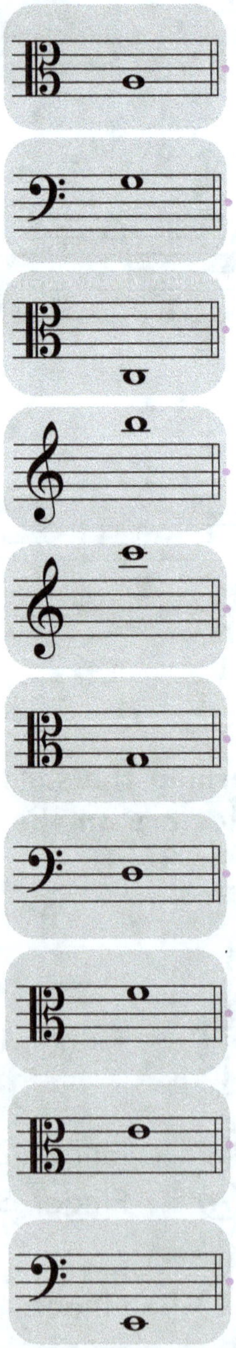

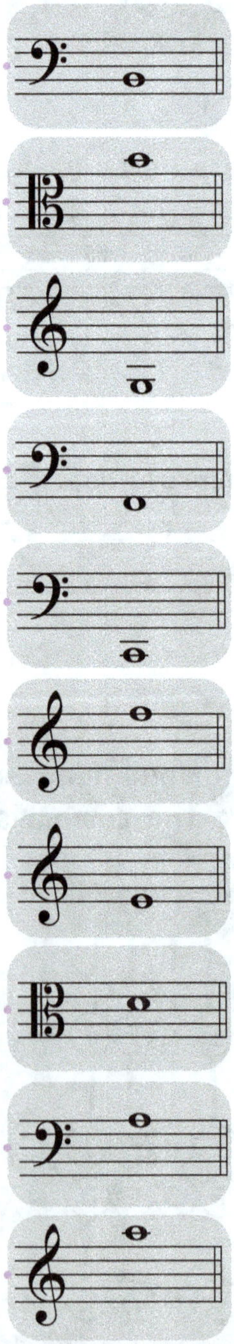

Time Signature

SIMPLE TIME	COMPOUND TIME
Simple and easier to count	More complex to count
Pulse can be divided into 2 beats	Pulse can be divided into 3 beats

Below are examples of the main beats in simple time.

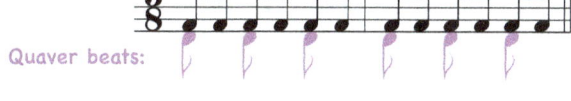

Crotchet beats: Minim beats:

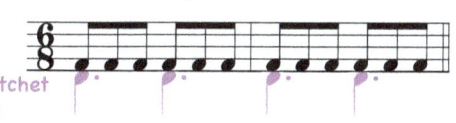

Quaver beats:

Below is an example of the main beats in compound time.

Dotted Crotchet beats:

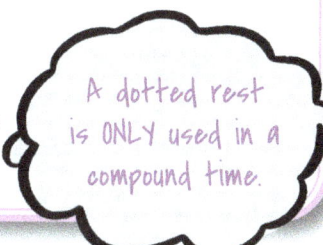

A dotted rest is ONLY used in a compound time.

Add a time signature to each rhythm accordingly and draw the appropriate beats of each bar.

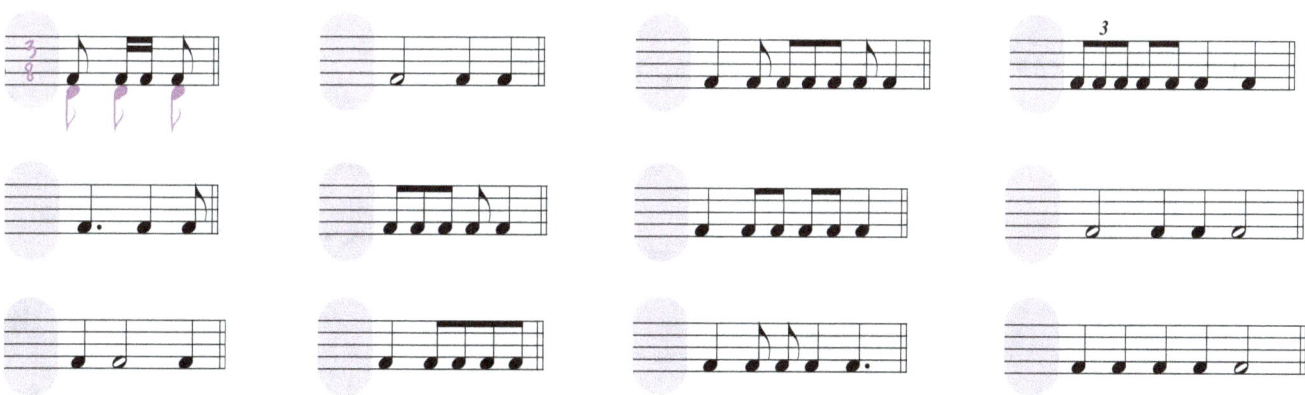

 From the exercise above, see if you can clap the rhythm with the metronome.
(Start with 60 beats per minute. Note that the metronome will be beating the beats which you have indicated while you clap the top rhythm.)

11

Duplets and Triplets

A Duplet is a pair of notes played in the time of three notes of the same value.

It is identified by a number '2' written above the grouped notes and is only used in compound time signatures. If there is no number 2, then it would not be considered as a duplet.

Below is the comparison between a duplet and triplet grouping.

DUPLET	TRIPLET
Used in Compound Time Signatures	Used in Simple Time Signatures
Beat is divided into TWO equal beats	Beat is divided into THREE equal beats
Eg.	Eg.

Below is an example of triplets in simple time.

Crotchet beats:

Below is an example of duplets in compound time.

Dotted Crotchet beats:

When writing a '2' on the notes, make sure it is over the beam of the notes.

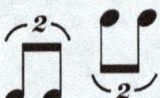

Duplet can also be written with a curved line that looks like a slur instead of a bracket as shown above.

1. Fill in the boxes with notes to complete the bars.

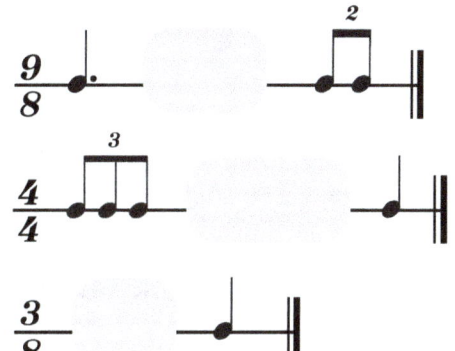
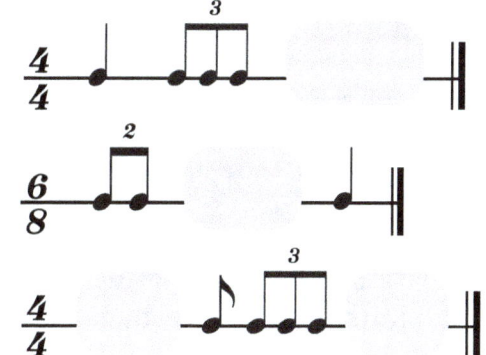

> For quaver note and rest grouping, remember to complete the beat first before moving onto the next beat.

2. Fill in the boxes with correctly grouped rests to complete the bars.

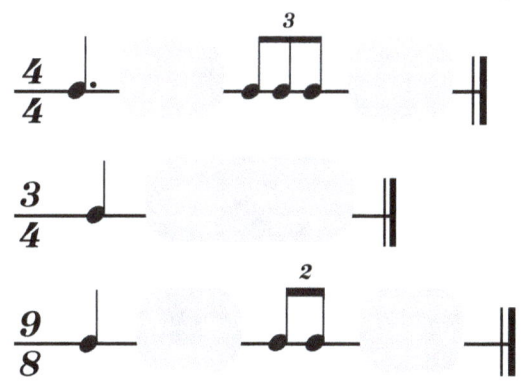
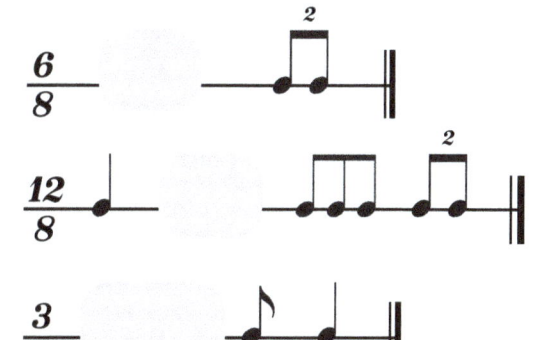

Rests in Quaver Triplet
In $\frac{3}{8}$ time, we use 2 quaver rests where there are 2 quaver beats of silence.

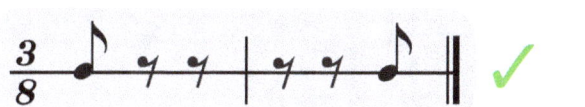 ✓ not  ✗

Sometimes we use rest(s) within a triplet within a simple time. Below is how they would look.

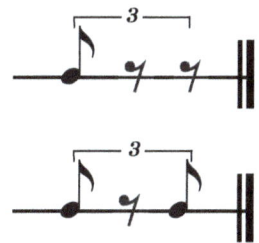
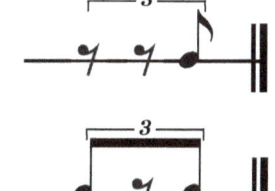
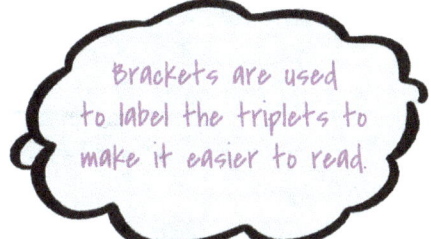

> Brackets are used to label the triplets to make it easier to read.

13

3. Write a 2 bar rhythm using the note and rest values which you have learnt. Include triplet(s) in each rhythm.

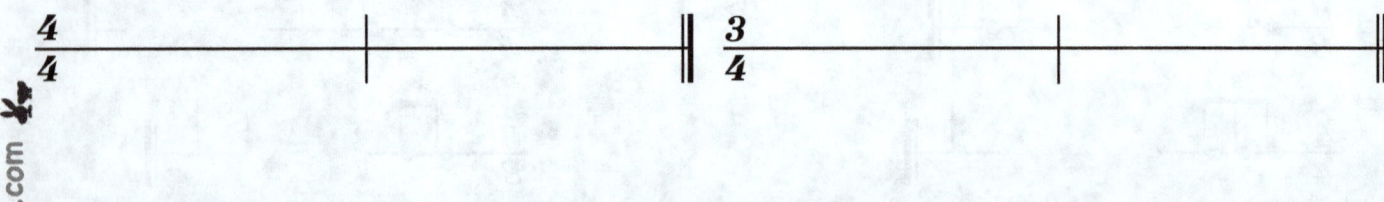

4. Write a 2 bar rhythm using the note and rest values which you have learnt. Include duplet(s) in each rhythm.

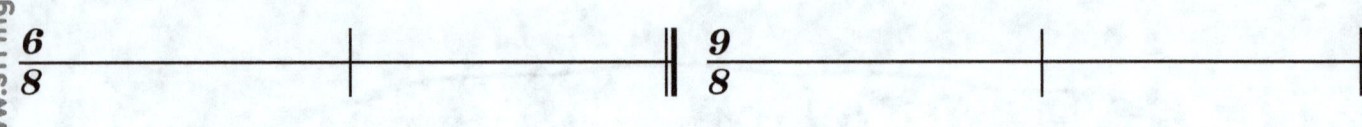

5. Match these boxes accordingly.

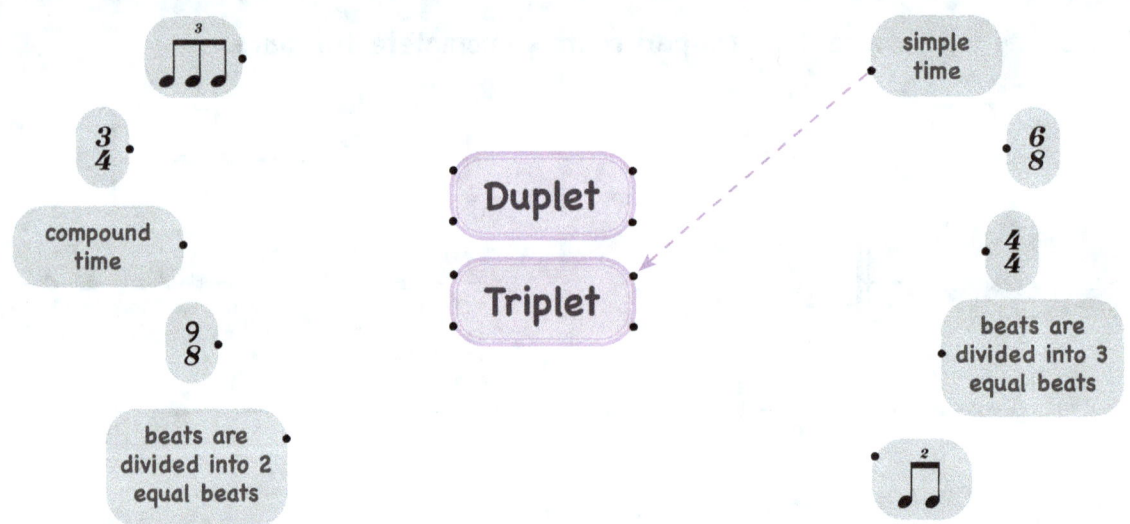

6. Add the correct time signature to the following rhythm.

Let us play and clap the rhythmic patterns in exercise 4.
Use a metronome if you need to help you keep in time.

Anacrusis

An anacrusis is a note or a few notes that come before the first bar. It can also be referred to as an upbeat.

As string players, we use an up-bow (∨) for a single up-beat note. This means that a down-bow (⊓) occurs on the first beat of the bar.

A - maz - ing — Grace! How sweet the sound

When you sing these tunes, notice how you emphasise the underlined words.

a- MAZ- ing   NOT   A-maz-ing   NOT   a-maz-ING

Words with more than one syllable are 'hyphenated' (place a dash separating the syllables)

The snow glows white on the moun-tain to-night; not a foot-print to be seen.

If there are more than a few words, say the words out loud and notice which word is more important so that you can emphasise it.

The SNOW   NOT   THE snow

Although it is not usually written, BAR ONE is ALWAYS the FIRST FULL bar of any music.

Occasionally when you have more than one upbeat note, they do not always start with the up-bow.

 Remember that the first beat of the first bar always starts with a down bow (⊓).

As shown below,

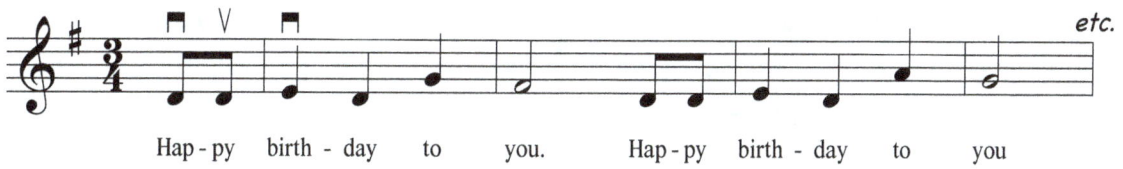

Hap - py birth - day to you. Hap - py birth - day to you

Notice that the last bar on all the lines on this topic is incomplete.
When a piece begins on an upbeat, the final bar has fewer beats than usual.
The amount of beats in the anacrusis is taken out of the last bar to even out
the difference as shown below.

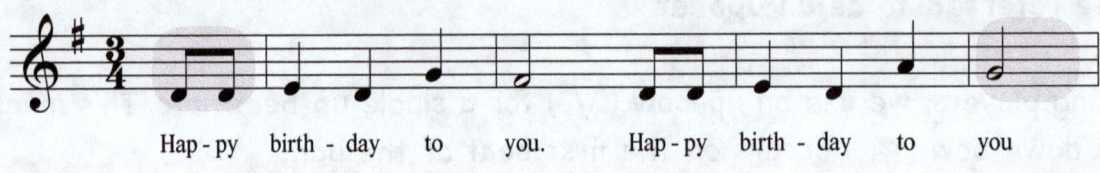

Hap - py birth - day to you.   Hap - py birth - day to you

The following rhythms begin with an anacrusis, but the note value in the last bar is
INCORRECT (too many beats). Rewrite the rhythm with the correct note or rest value on
the last bar.

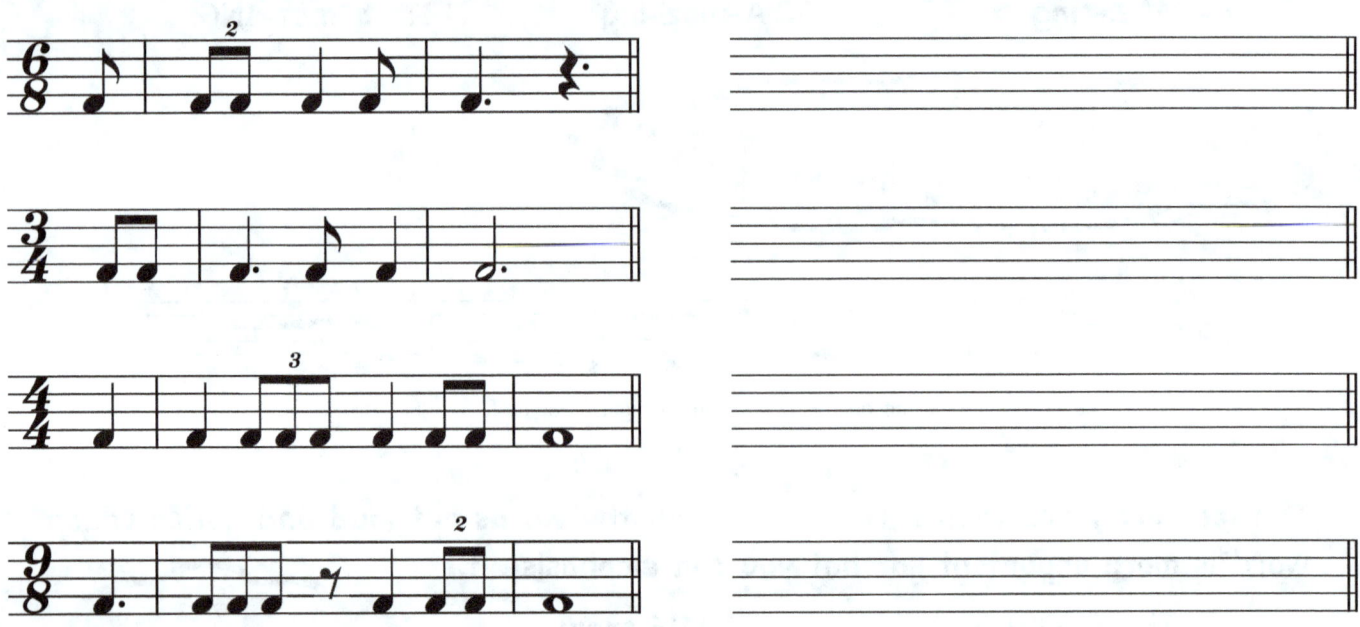

Finding emphasised (important) words.
Let us go back to the "Amazing Grace" song. Say the words out loud to find
those important words or syllables.

A - maz - ing— Grace! How sweet the sound

Notice that the important words are recognised as the main beats of each
bar. Emphasising words helps composers write music. For a singer, it gives
more character to the song.

Creating a Rhythm to a Given Couplet

Writing rhythmic pattern to a couplet of words.
A couplet is two lines of poetry which typically rhyme and are of the same length.

> The street cars are like frosted cupcakes.
> All covered up with cold snowflakes.
>
>   - Dorothy Aldis

1. Read the words out loud and underline the emphasised word or syllable. The word or syllable emphasised is usually the 1st beat of the bar.

    The <u>street</u> cars are <u>like</u> frosted <u>cup</u>cakes.
    All <u>cov</u>ered up <u>with</u> cold <u>snow</u>flakes.

    *(Notice how the first emphasis is on the word 'street'.
    This means that this couplet has an anacrusis.)*

    Stick notation
    We take the traditional notes and remove the notehead ♩ = | or ♫ = ⊓.

    We still use the note heads when using minim, dotted minim, or semibreve notes ♩, ♩., or o.

    The rests are still written the same way.

2. Tap the beat and read the words out.
   Using stick notation, write out the rhythm on top of the words.

    Example A:

        | | | | | | | ♩
    The <u>street</u> cars are <u>like</u> frosted <u>cup</u>cakes.
        | | | | | | ♩.
    All <u>cov</u>ered up <u>with</u> cold <u>snow</u>flakes.

3. **Tap the beat using your fingers** (using your thumb as the main beat of each bar and your other) **to help you decide which time signature to use.**

This is how the rhythm would look using $\frac{3}{4}$ time.

⚠️ Remember to deduct the value of the anacrusis from the last bar!

17

another way of writing the rhythm is as below...

Example B:

The street cars are like frosted cupcakes.

All covered up with cold snowflakes.

The street cars are like fros-ted cup-cakes. All co-vered up with cold snow-flakes.

1. Write a suitable rhythmic pattern to the following couplet.
   - Write the words clearly under the notes (Give yourself room to write the words.)
   - Use hyphens for words of more than one syllable

   Jack fell down and broke his crown,

   And Jill came tumbling after.

   I never saw a purple cow,

   I never hope to see one.

2. Using TWO different time signatures, write TWO different rhythmic patterns to the following couplet.

> Hear the honking of the goose,
>
> I think he's angry at the moose.

> Bobby Shaftoe's gone to sea,
>
> Silver buckles on his knee.

Key Signature

In Grade 2, we looked at different ways of working out and memorizing the key signature.

A. **FORWARD and BACKWARD TABLE**
Remember that SHARP is higher *(forward)* and FLAT is lower (backward). All we have to do is remember the first 2 scales in order and alternate the letters forwards.

1. Fill in the blanks where needed.

A   B   C   D   E   F   G   A   B   C

NO.	SHARPS	SCALE
0	-	C major
1	F♯	G major
2	F♯, C♯	
3		
4		
5		
6		
7		

NO.	FLATS	SCALE
0	-	C major
1	B♭	F major
2	B♭, E♭	
3		
4		
5		
6		
7		

B. Circle of fifths (commonly used)

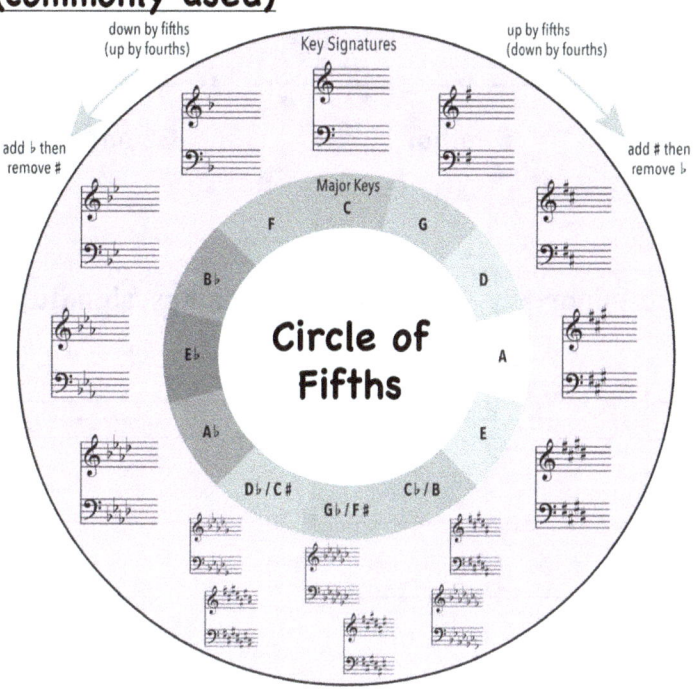

C. Acronyms

Fat **C**at **G**ives **D**ad **A**n **E**njoyable **B**agel. **(SHARPS)**
Before **E**ating **A** **D**onut **G**et **C**hocolate **F**irst. **(FLATS)**

2. Draw all the sharps and flats on both clefs in the correct order. Do this without refering to the above.

 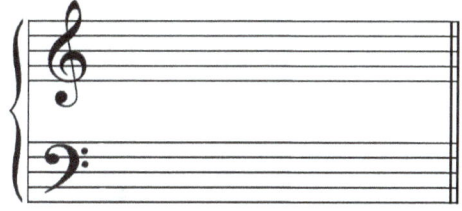

This is how the key signature would be written using the alto clef.

3. Copy the sharps and flats for the alto clef as shown above.

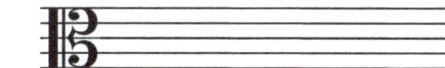 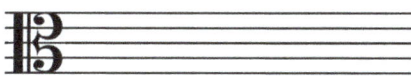

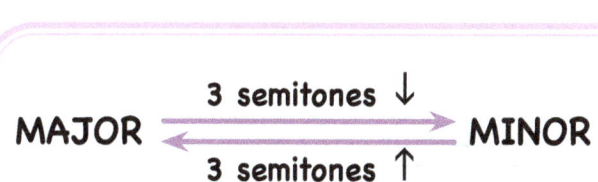

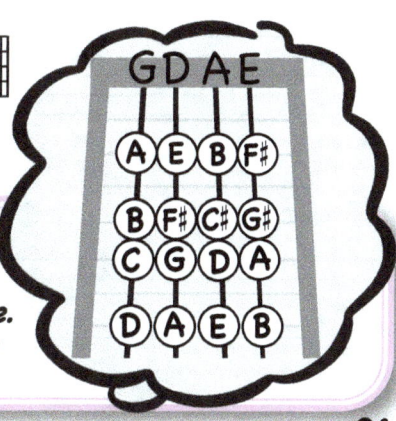

Refer to your fingerboard in 1st position for reference. (photo on the right is the violin's fingerboard)

21

4. Draw each key signature in the correct order.

5. Name the major and minor key for each of these key signatures.

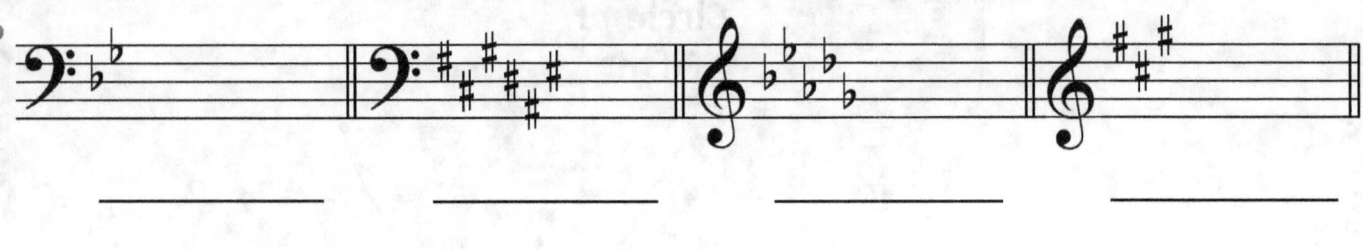

6. Using minim notes, draw the key signature and notes of the arpeggio in an ascending and descending order of these scales.

7. What is the difference between these THREE minor scales and how should you play them?

NATURAL MINOR	No change. Play the notes according to the key signature.
HARMONIC MINOR	
MELODIC MINOR	

8. Add a clef and any accidentals necessary to make each of the scale below. Mark each tone with a slur.

G harmonic minor

A major

G melodic minor

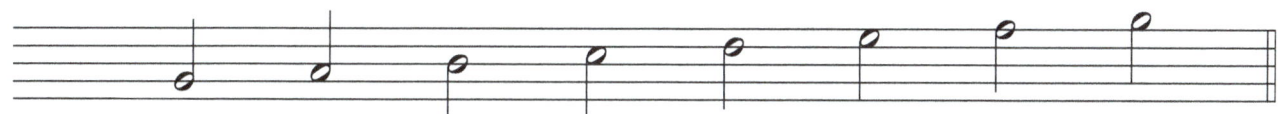

D major

B harmonic minor

G major

9. Write out these scales accordingly.

E♭ major
- Draw a treble clef
- Use accidentals
- One octave descending only
- Use crotchet notes
- Mark each semitone with a slur
- Complete the scale with a double bar line

E harmonic minor
- Draw a bass clef
- Use accidentals
- One octave in an ascending and descending order
- Use minim notes
- Mark each tone with a slur
- Complete the scale with a double bar line

G harmonic minor
- Draw a treble clef
- Use key signature
- One octave in an ascending and descending order
- Use semibreve notes
- Mark each tone with a slur
- Complete the scale with a double bar line

B major
- Draw an alto clef
- Use key signature
- One octave in a descending and ascending order
- Use quaver notes in pairs
- Mark each semitone with a slur
- Complete the scale with a double bar line

Scale Degrees

A <u>Scale</u> is a group of notes starting from the name of the note of the scale that are arranged by ascending or descending order of pitch.

In grade 1 and 2, we looked into the difference between a major and minor scale with a major sounding happy and minor scales sound sad. We also described each scale degree of those scales with 1 being the tonic note.

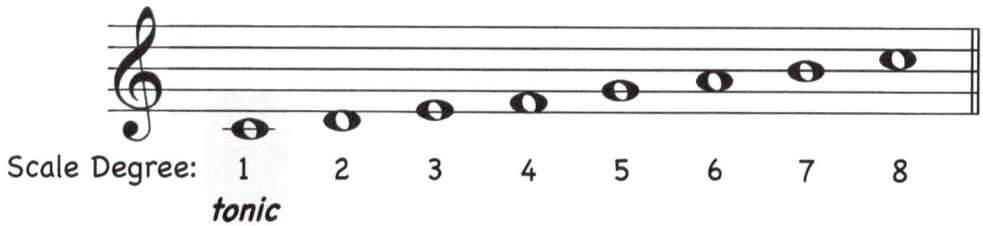

Each scale degree has a special technical name besides the tonic which we will learn here.

Scale Degree	Technical Name	Solfege Name	Hint Of Remembering
1 or 8	Tonic	Do	Learnt in Grade 1. Most important degree. 1st and 8th note is the same note name. Hence they are both considered Tonic.
2	Supertonic	Re	"Super" in Latin means above
3	Mediant	Mi	Doh-Reh-Mediant
4	Subdominant	Fa	"Sub" in Latin means under, which is a noe below Dominant (Dominant's sidekick)
5	Dominant	Sol	2nd most important. Think - It's easier to hold something firmly with 5 fingers than fewer.
6	Submediant	La	("Sub" = under , "Mediant" = 3rd) A 3rd or 3 steps below a Tonic note.
7	Leading Note	Ti	Leads to the Tonic

If you have not already, we recommend that you watch the Sound of Music (1965) movie or just listen to the song "Do-Re-Mi".

Another way of remembering the names of the scale degree, is by using acronyms as shown below.

To **S**hear **M**ore **S**heep, **D**on't **S**ay **L**ION!!

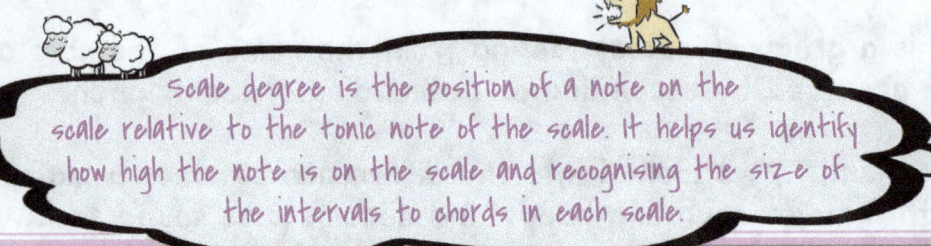

Scale degree is the position of a note on the scale relative to the tonic note of the scale. It helps us identify how high the note is on the scale and recognising the size of the intervals to chords in each scale.

1. The notes below are all from the C major scale. Identify the correct scale degree name under each note.

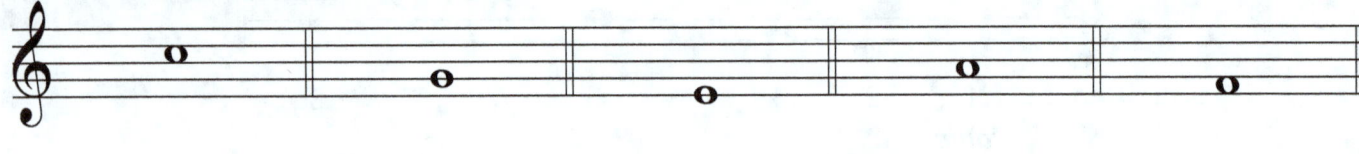

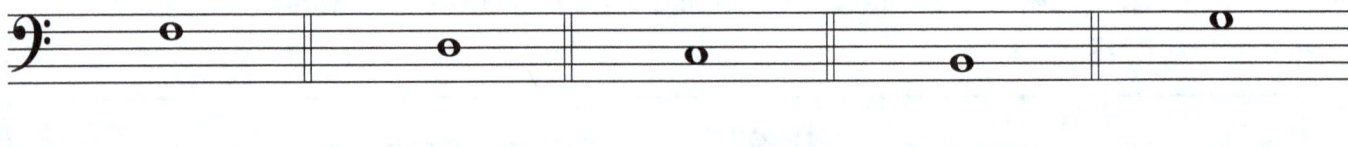

2. Without looking back on your notes, write out the correct technical names for these scale degrees.

1	2	3	4	5	6	7
Tonic						

3. Name the following major key and the technical scale degree name of each note.

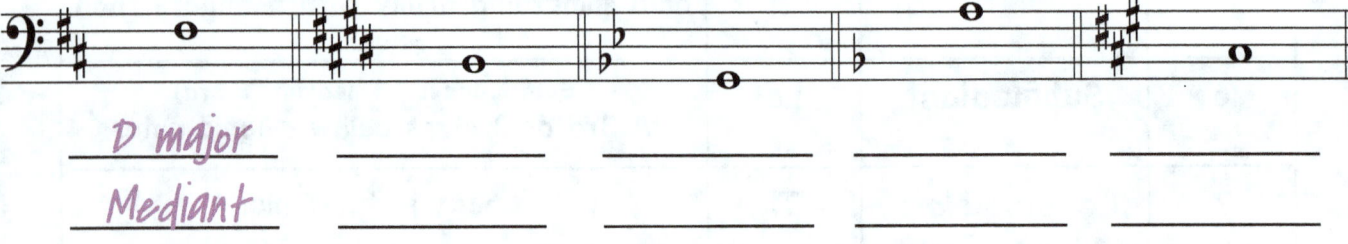

D major
Mediant

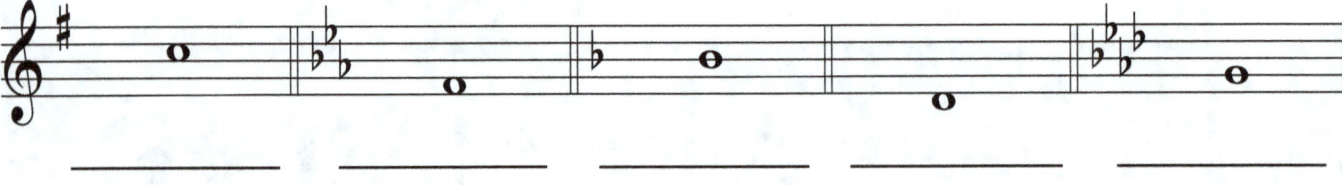

Leading Note also occurs in minor scales (harmonic and melodic) **however the 7th note would have to be raised.**

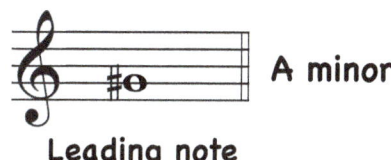

A minor

Leading note

SUBTONIC (7th)
Remember that "sub" means under.
Subtonic is in replacement of the leading note when you are looking at the note from a natural minor scale where the 7th note is lowered.

4. Name the following minor key and the technical scale degree name of each note.

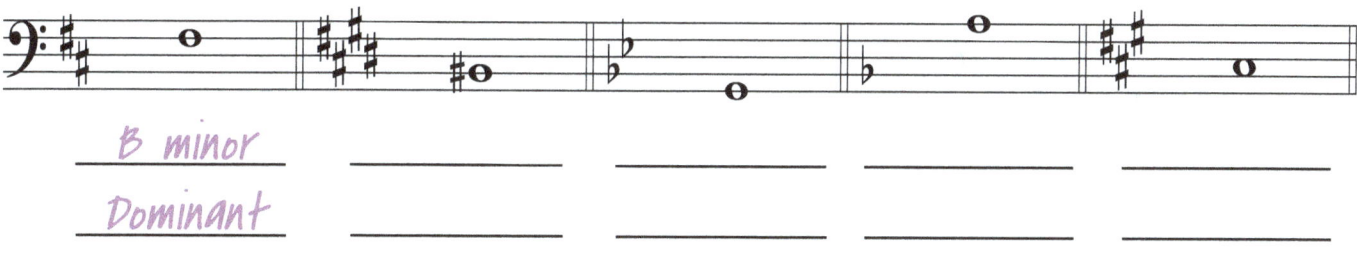

B minor
Dominant

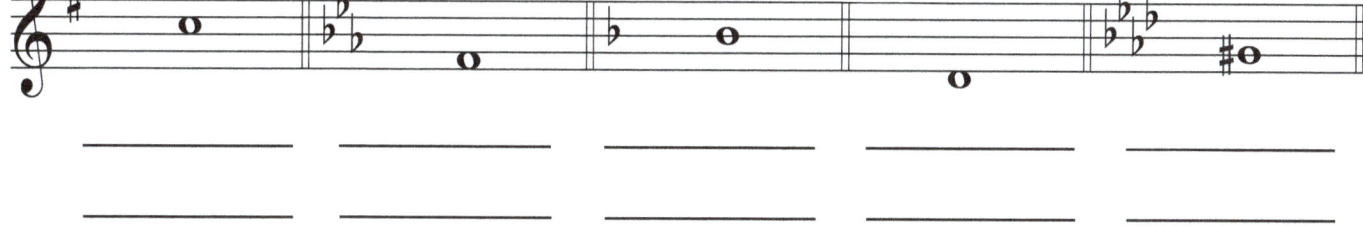

5. Draw the correct key signatures and note of these scale degrees.

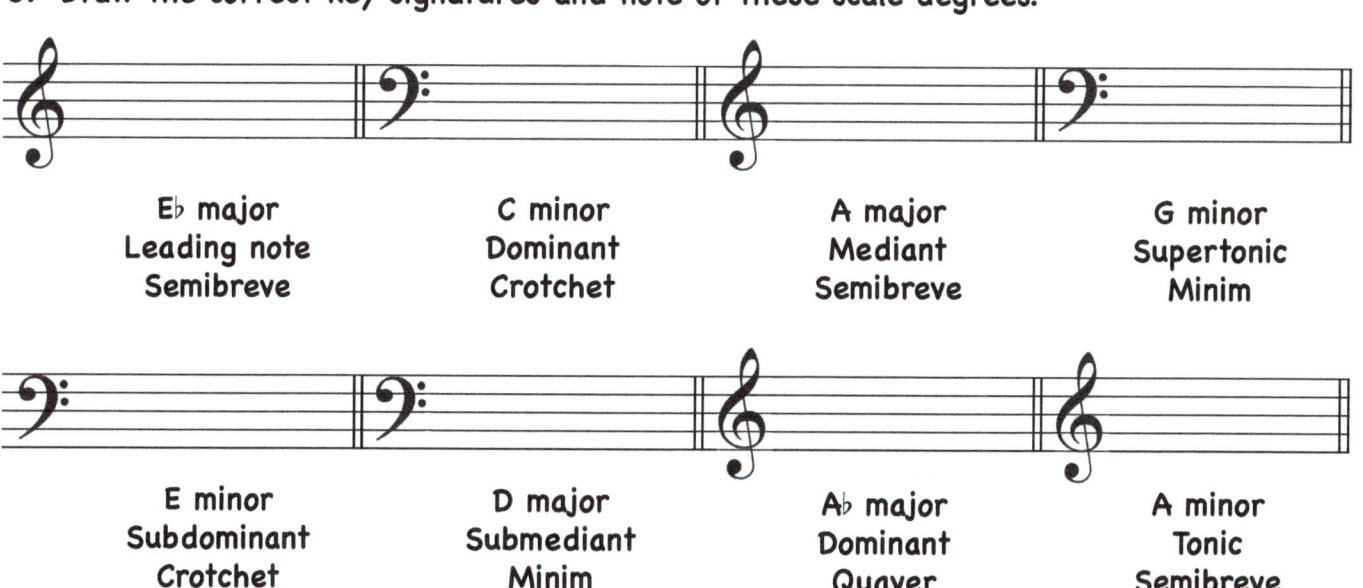

E♭ major
Leading note
Semibreve

C minor
Dominant
Crotchet

A major
Mediant
Semibreve

G minor
Supertonic
Minim

E minor
Subdominant
Crotchet

D major
Submediant
Minim

A♭ major
Dominant
Quaver

A minor
Tonic
Semibreve

27

Tiny Revision

1. **Draw these notes at the same pitch on the alto clef.**
   Remember where the middle C is on the alto clef.

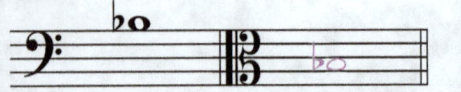  

2. **Draw ONE note that is equal to the total value of the note of each bar.**

3. **Add the time signature to each of the following rhythms.**

4. **Fill in the boxes with notes to complete the bars.**

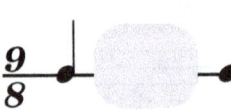    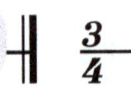 

5. **Draw all the sharps and flats on all clefs in the correct order.**

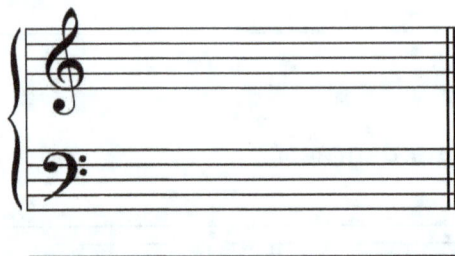
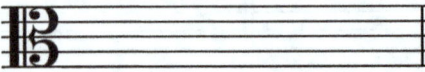
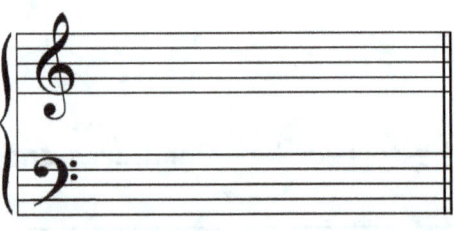
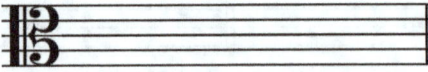

6. **Write a suitable rhythmic pattern to the following couplet.**
   Write the words clearly under the notes and use hyphens for words of more than one syllable.

   Jack be nimble, Jack be quick,

   Jack jumped over the candlestick.

28

7. Write a 2 bar rhythm using the note and rest values which you have learnt. Include triplet(s) in each rhythm.

$\frac{4}{4}$ ‖ $\frac{3}{4}$ ‖

8. Add a clef and any accidentals necessary to these scales. Mark each tone with a slur.

G melodic minor

E♭ major

9. Write the scale of E♭ major
   - Draw a bass clef
   - Use accidentals
   - One octave in a descending order
   - Use minim notes
   - Mark each tone with a slur
   - Complete the scale with a double bar line

10. Without looking back on your notes, write out the correct technical names for these scale degrees.

1	2	3	4	5	6	7
Tonic						

11. Draw the correct key sigantures and note of these scale degrees.

E minor   E♭ major   F♯ minor   D major
Supertonic   Tonic   Mediant   Leading note
Crotchet   Minim   Semibreve   Semibreve

29

Intervals & their Quality

In Grade 3, we will continue identifying the quality of the interval.

 Bottom note is the tonic or 1. ALWAYS count from the bottom note.
When the upper note is found in the major scale of the bottom note the interval is called MAJOR or PERFECT.

Harmonic	Melodic
Notes sit on top of each other	Notes sit next to each other
Played together at the same time (Harmonize)	Played one after the other (Melody/Tune)
Eg. Perfect 5th 1 2 3 4 **5**	Eg. Perfect 5th 1 2 3 4 **5**

PERFECT - unison, 4th, 5th, 8ve

1. Circle the intervals that are of PERFECT quality.

1. Name the interval, its quality, and note if they are a harmonic or melodic interval.

minor 3rd
harmonic

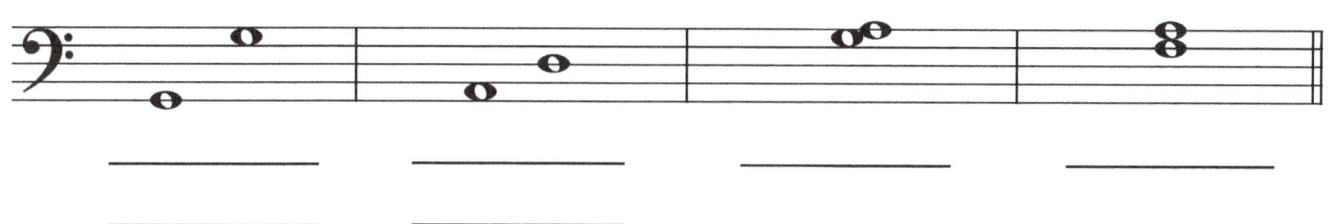

2. Draw the following harmonic intervals above the given tonic notes.

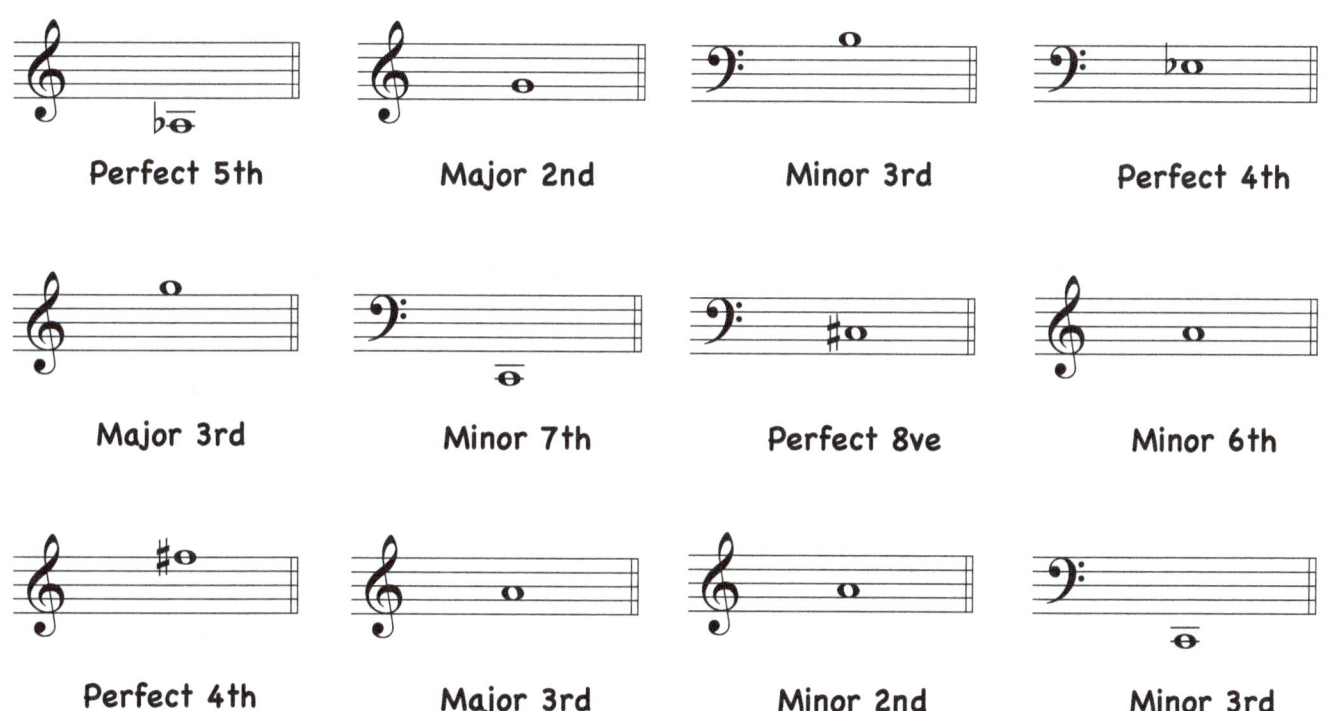

Perfect 5th — Major 2nd — Minor 3rd — Perfect 4th

Major 3rd — Minor 7th — Perfect 8ve — Minor 6th

Perfect 4th — Major 3rd — Minor 2nd — Minor 3rd

3. Draw the following melodic intervals above the given tonic notes.

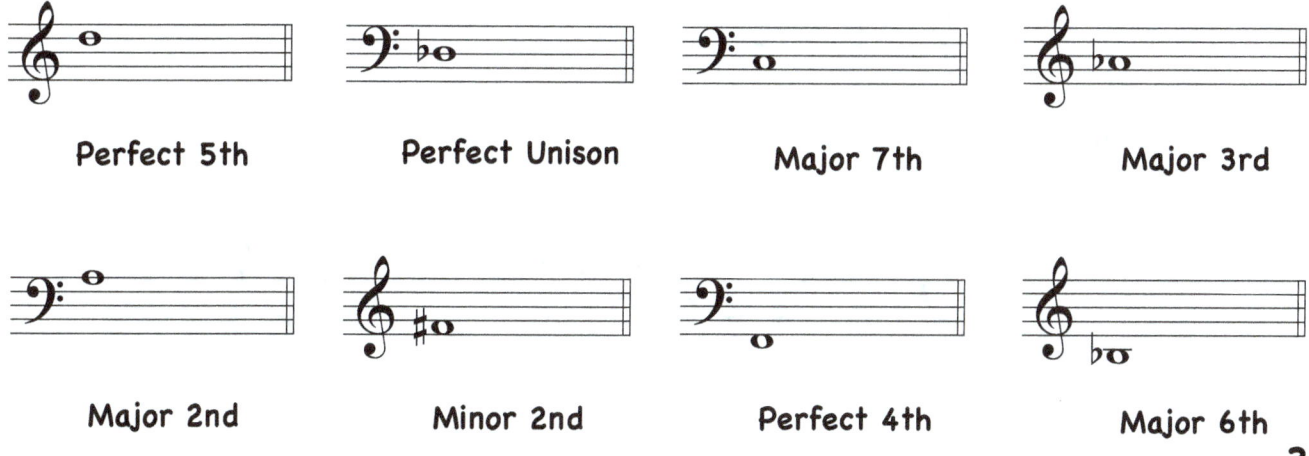

Perfect 5th — Perfect Unison — Major 7th — Major 3rd

Major 2nd — Minor 2nd — Perfect 4th — Major 6th

31

Dominant Triads

A <u>chord</u> is two or more notes played at the same time.

A <u>triad</u> is a chord made up of notes of an arpeggio of a scale.
(1st, 3rd, and 5th degree notes of the scale.)

As shown below, in a MAJOR scale, triads are built on the tonic (1st) and dominant (5th) notes.

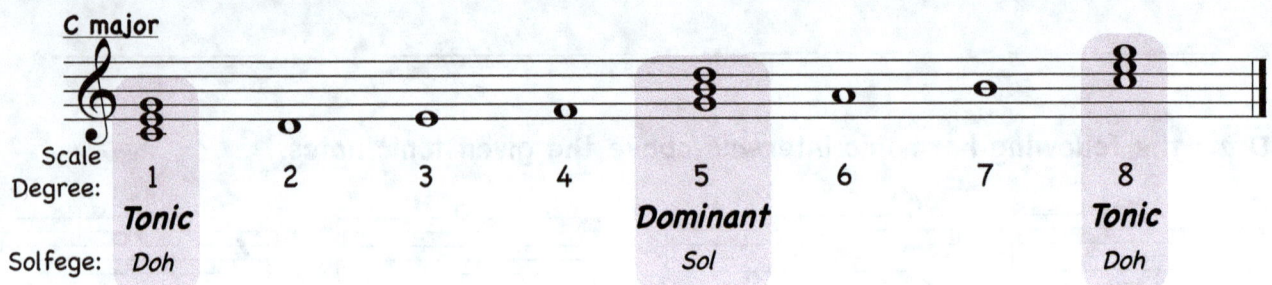

Scale degree is ALWAYS counted starting from the bottom upwards.

There are other ways of labeling the tonic and dominant triads in a major key.

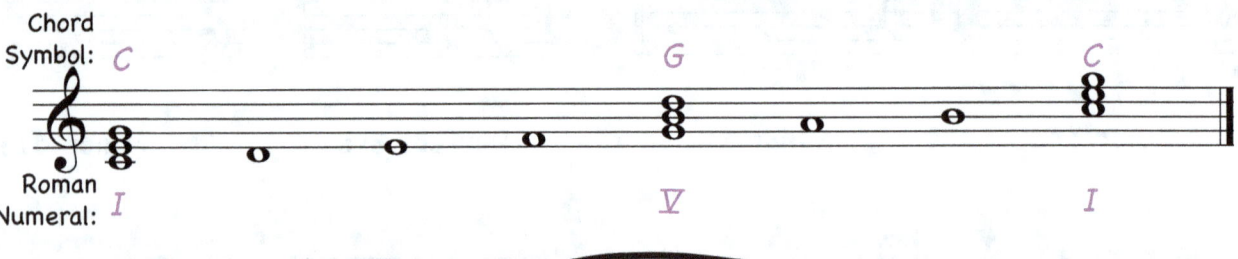

MAJOR triads
ROMAN NUMERAL - ALL in capital letters (eg. I or V)
CHORD SYMBOL - All capital letters (eg. A)

1. Using semibreve notes, draw the key signatures and dominant triads in these major keys.

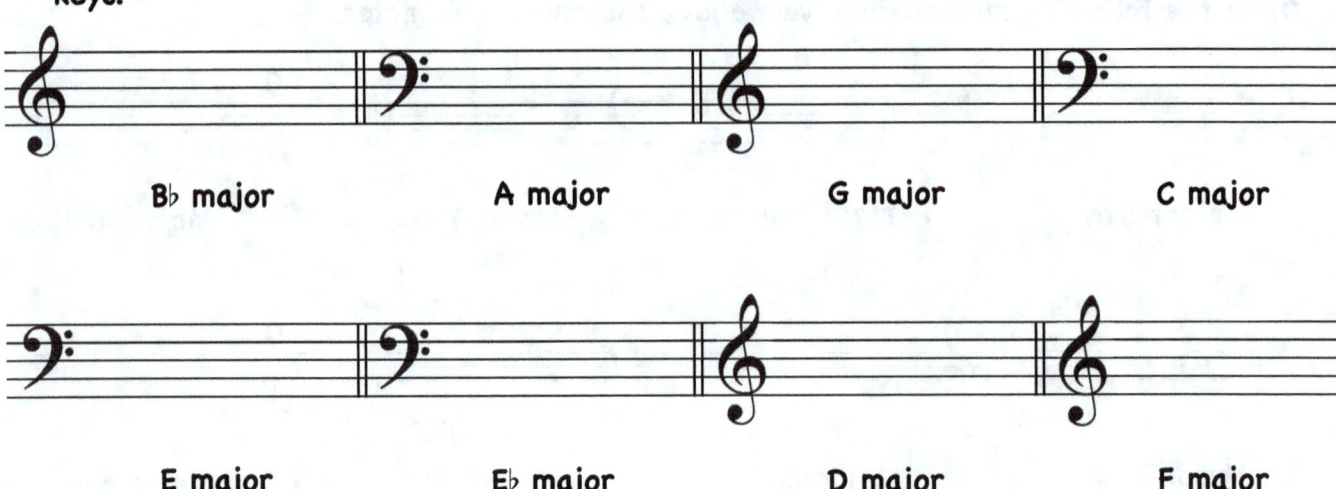

2. Name these major scales and write triads on the tonic and dominant scale degrees.

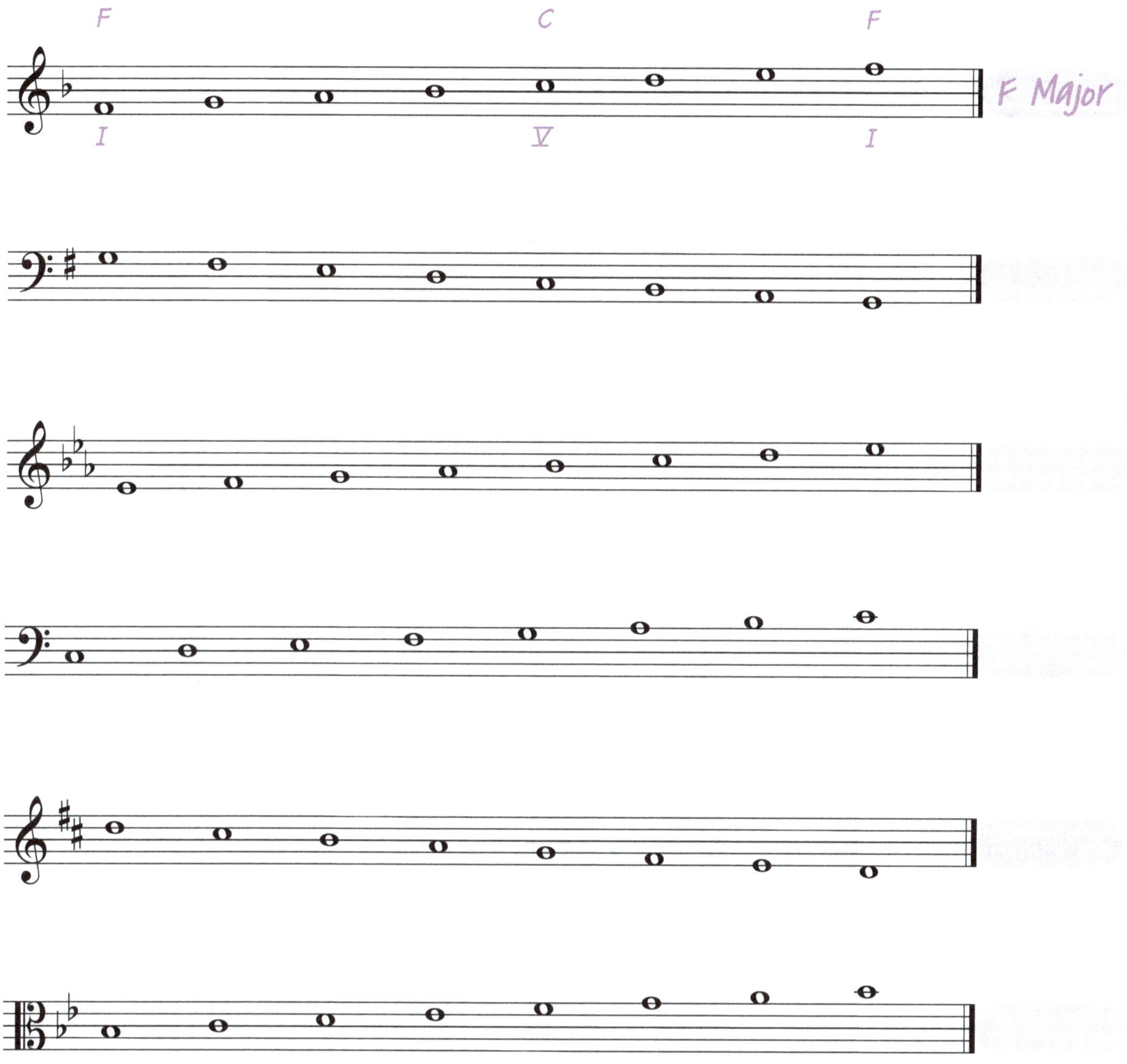

F   C   F

F Major

I   V   I

3. Label the triads in exercise No. 2 using chord symbols.
 Chord symbols are to be written ABOVE the stave.

4. Label the triads in exercise No. 2 using Roman Numerals.
 Roman Numerals are to be written UNDER the stave.

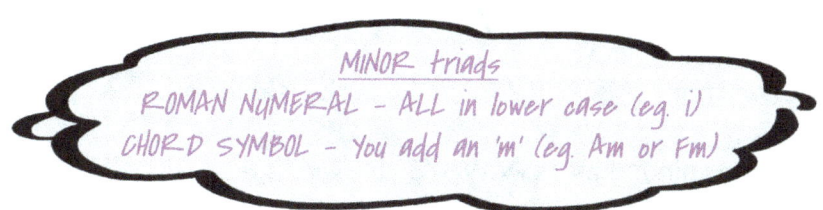

MINOR triads
ROMAN NUMERAL - ALL in lower case (eg. i)
CHORD SYMBOL - You add an 'm' (eg. Am or Fm)

Below in the scale of a MINOR scale, triads are built on the tonic (1st) and dominant (5th) notes.

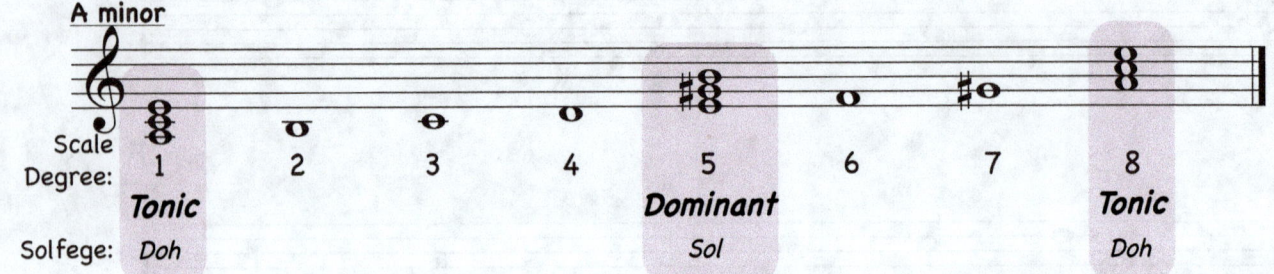

There are other ways of labeling the tonic and dominant triads in a minor key.

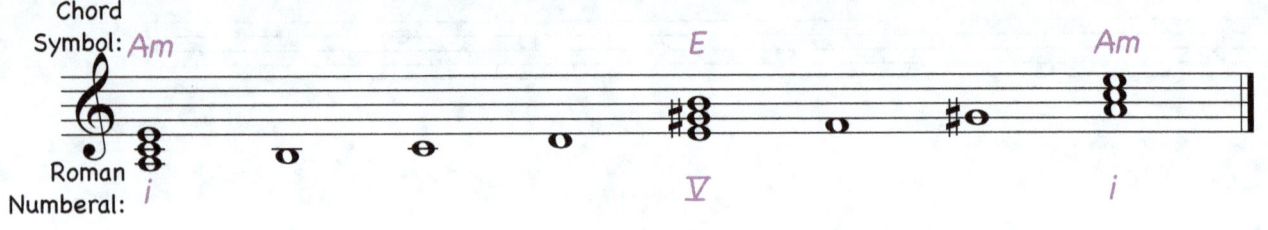

Dominant chord in a <u>MINOR</u> key is ALWAYS <u>MAJOR</u> because the 7th note (leading note) is ALWAYS raised a semitone.

5. Using semibreve notes, draw the key signature and dominant triads in these minor keys.

6. Cross out the incorrect answers.

A. Roman Numerals are written   ABOVE / BELOW   the stave.

B. Chord Symbols are written   ABOVE / BELOW   the stave.

C. The dominant triad in a minor key is ALWAYS a   MAJOR / MINOR   triad.

34

7. When counting the scale degree of a scale, always start counting, starting from the _____ upwards.

8. In a minor key, what letter do you add when labeling triads using chord symbols? _____ .

9. Name these minor scales and in semibreves, write out the tonic and dominant triads.

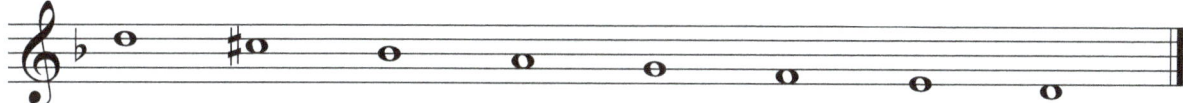

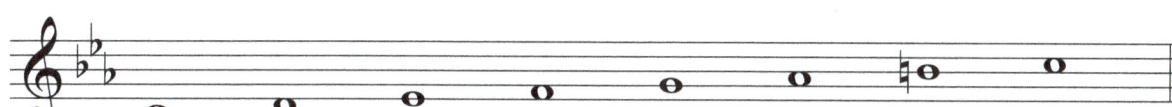

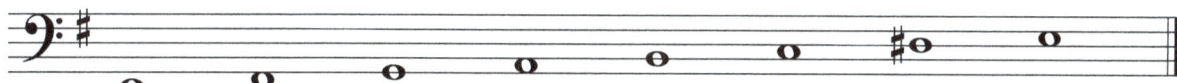

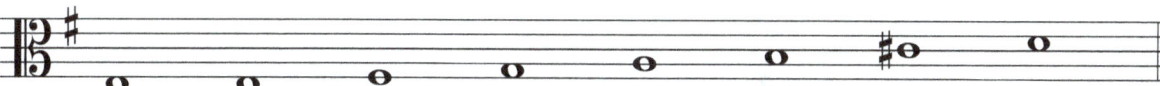

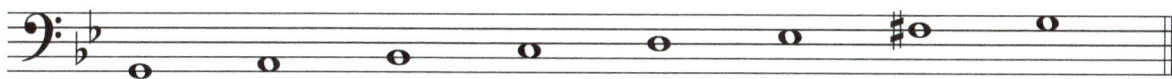

10. Label the triads in exercise No. 9 using Roman Numerals and chord symbols.

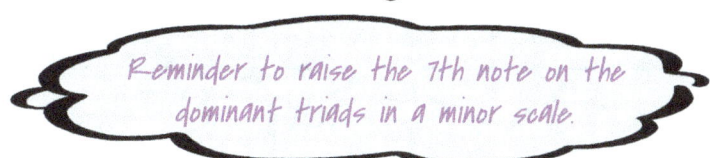

Reminder to raise the 7th note on the dominant triads in a minor scale.

Primary Triads

In grade 3, we will look into three PRIMARY triads: Tonic (I), Subdominant (IV), and Dominant (V) triad in a major and minor key.

1	4	5
Tonic i I	Subdominant iv IV	Dominant V (always a major chord)

When you write chords, your root note of each chord can be written any where on the stave. Below shows how these triads look in a major key.

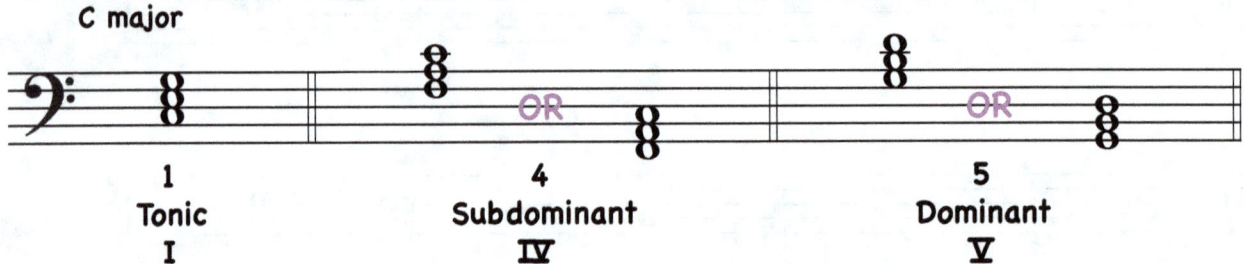

C major

1 — Tonic — I
4 — Subdominant — IV
5 — Dominant — V

Below shows how these triads look in a minor key.

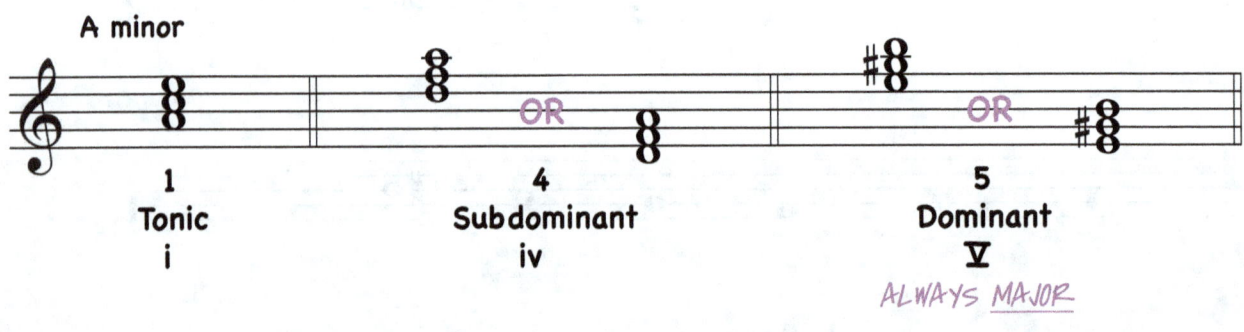

A minor

1 — Tonic — i
4 — Subdominant — iv
5 — Dominant — V   ALWAYS MAJOR

1. Name the THREE primary triads using their technical names.

TECHNICAL NAME			

2. Using Roman Numerals, what are the THREE primary triads of a major and minor key?

MAJOR KEY			
MINOR KEY			

36

3. Using semibreve notes, write out the primary triads of these major and minor keys.

G major

B♭ major

B minor

F♯ minor

F major

A minor

4. In semibreves, write out the primary triads of these scales.

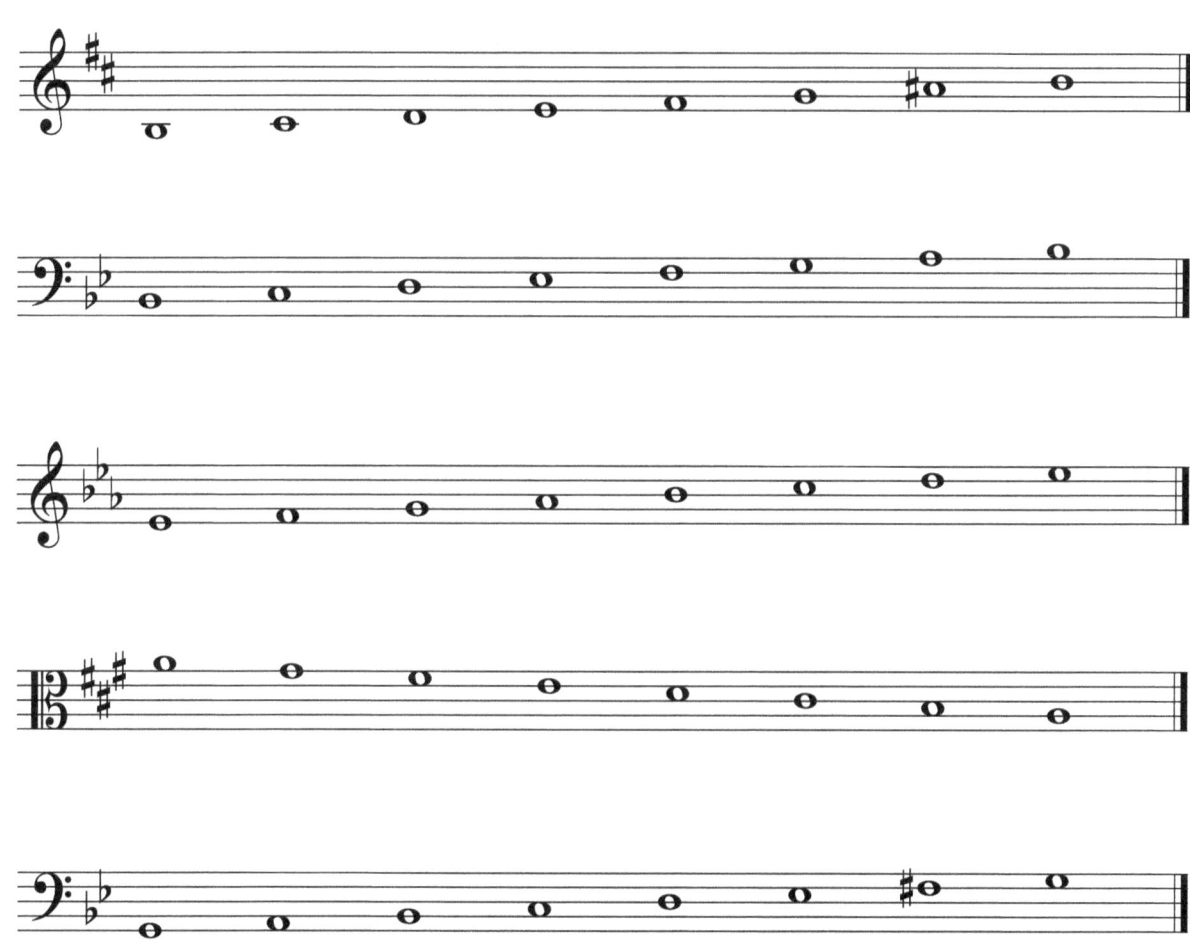

5. Label the primary triads in exercise No. 4 using Roman Numerals and chord symbols.

Chord Progression

Chord Progression means an order in which chords move from one to another within a piece of music.

1. Using Roman Numerals, label the triads under these chords to show the chord progression.

2. Using chord symbols, label the triads above the chords to show the chord progression.

2nd Inversion

Let us revise the major tonic triads which we have learnt in Grade 1.

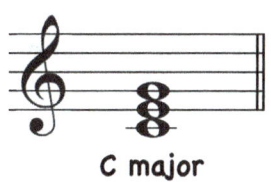
C major
Tonic triad

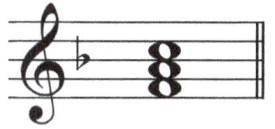
F major
Tonic triad

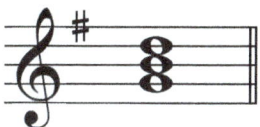
G major
Tonic triad

The tonic triads above are called root position.
(The tonic note is at the bottom of the triad.)

The word inversion is when we invert the triad by taking the note which is at the bottom of the triad and place it up an octave.

Eg.

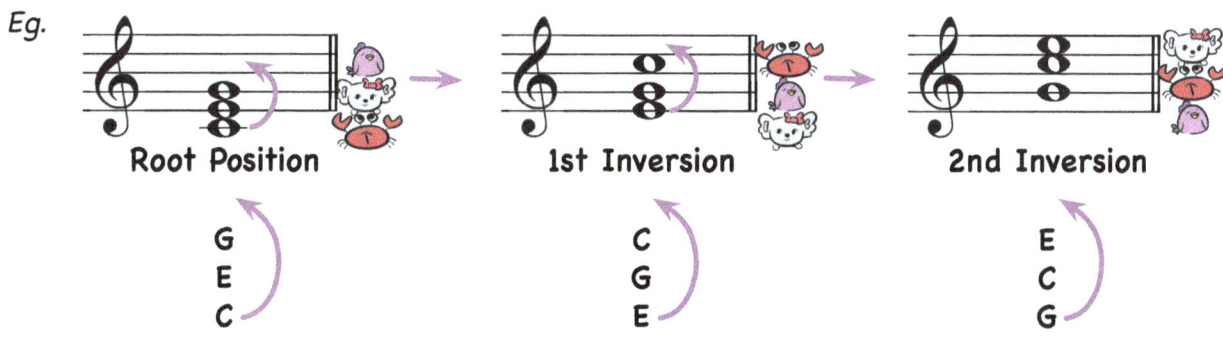

Root Position   1st Inversion   2nd Inversion

G   C   E
E   G   C
C   E   G

1st inversion: Take the bottom note of the tonic triad and place it on the top.

2nd inversion: Take 2 notes from the bottom of the tonic triad and place it on the top.

1. Using letters, arrange the notes of these root position chords in the 1st and 2nd inversion.

KEY, ROOT POSITION	1ST INVERSION	2ND INVERSION
E minor (B / G / E)		
B♭ major (F / D / B♭)		

KEY, ROOT POSITION	1ST INVERSION	2ND INVERSION
A major (E / C# / A)		
G minor (D / B♭ / G)		

2. Using semibreve notes, write the tonic triad in root position of each key and then write its 1st inversion. (Take care of the clefs.)

Eg. E minor 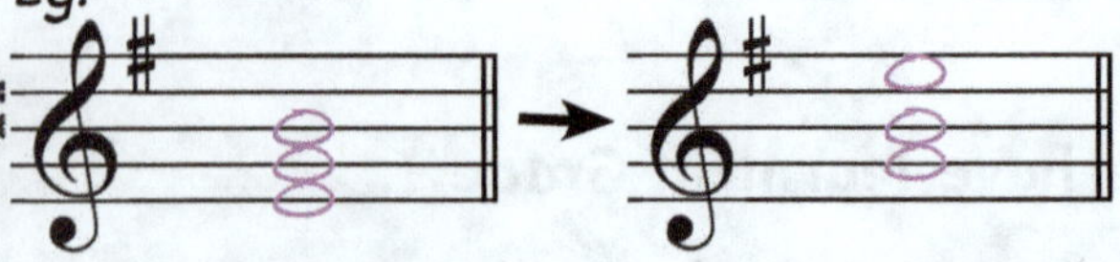
Root Position → 1st Inversion

3. G major 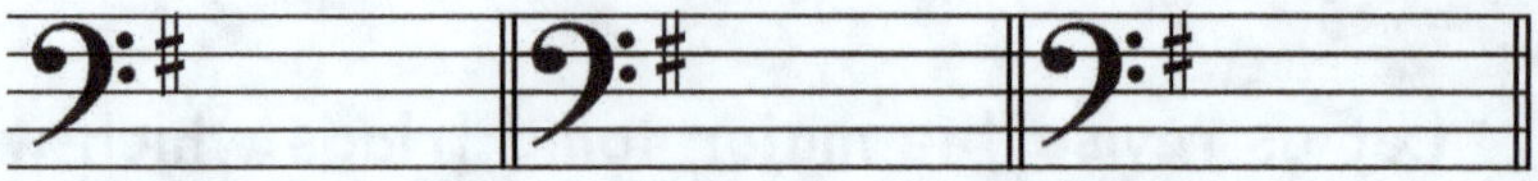
Root Position   1st Inversion   2nd Inversion

1. B♭ major 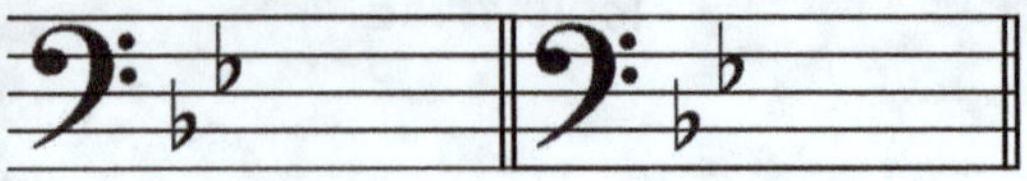
Root Position   1st Inversion

4. F♯ minor 
Root Position   1st Inversion   2nd Inversion

2. A minor 
Root Position   1st Inversion

5. F major 
Root Position   1st Inversion   2nd Inversion

> Although the notes of a chord are inverted, the note names are still the same as the original chord.

3. Using semibreve notes, use the appropriate key signature and triads accordingly for each of the following keys.

E major
Dominant
1st inversion

F♯ minor
Tonic
Root position

A♭ major
Subdominant
1st inversion

D minor
Dominant
2nd inversion

E♭ major
Tonic
2nd inversion

B minor
Subdominant
1st inversion

B major
Dominant
Root position

C minor
Dominant
Root position

Writing a Bass Line

1. **Use a single root note of each triad shown by the Roman Numerals to write the bass line.**

    Take note of the time signature.

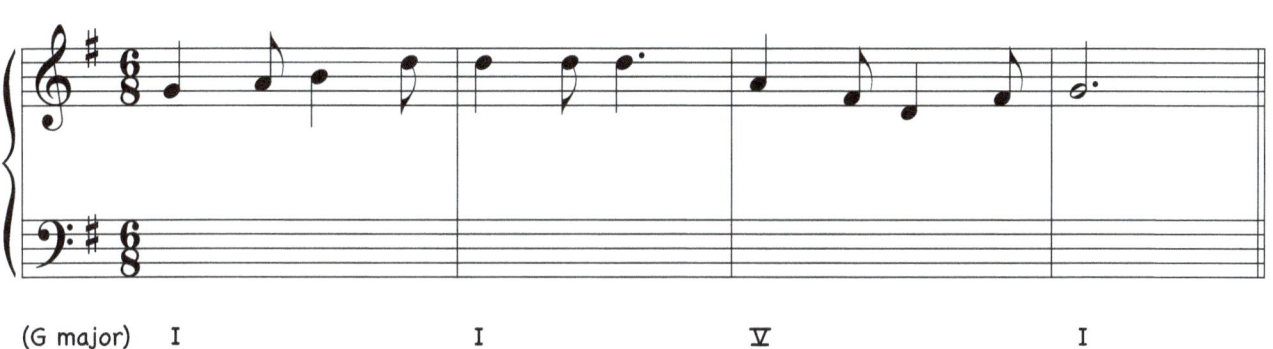

(G major)   I   I   V   I

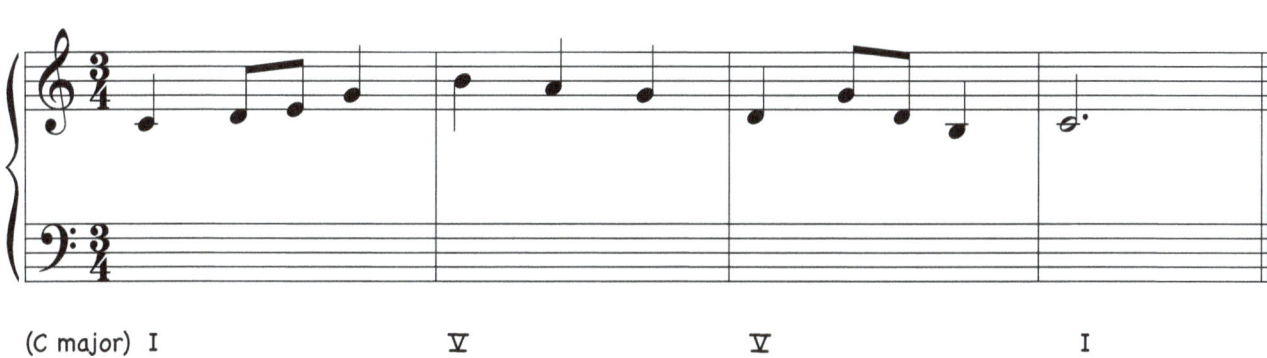

(C major)   I   V   V   I

(E minor)   i   i   V   i

(D major)   I   I   V   I

2. **Use a single root note of each triad shown by the chord symbols to write the bass line.**

Composition

1. Write a tune using notes from the tonic or dominant triads shown by the Roman numerals in these major and minor keys.

   Start and end on a tonic note.

2. **Write a tune using notes from the tonic or dominant triads shown by the chord symbols in these major and minor keys.**

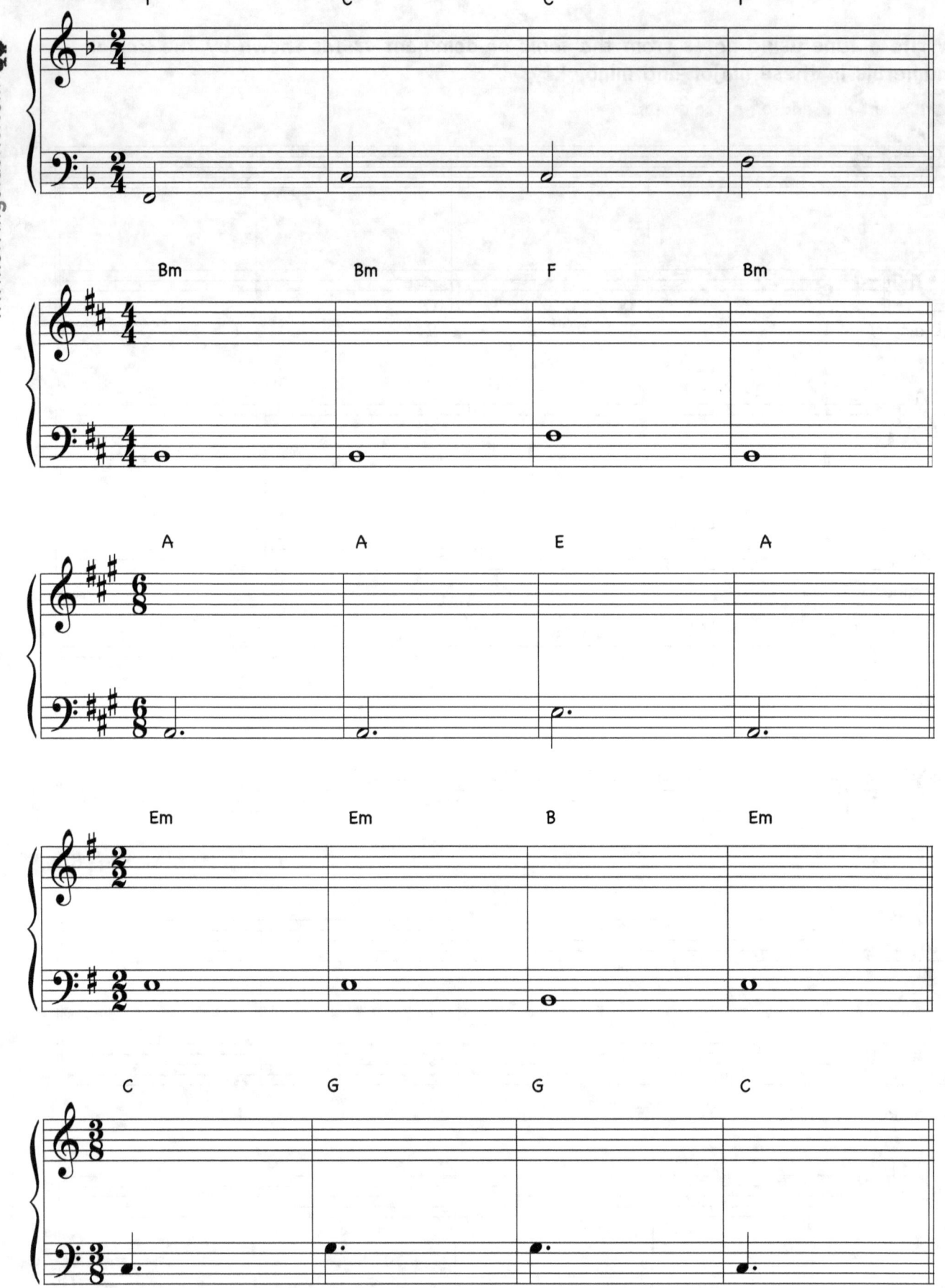

Real and Tonal Sequences

A <u>sequence</u> is a melodic pattern that is repeated starting on a different note each time either moving the whole pattern upwards or downwards.

Below shows the TWO different kind of sequence we can use

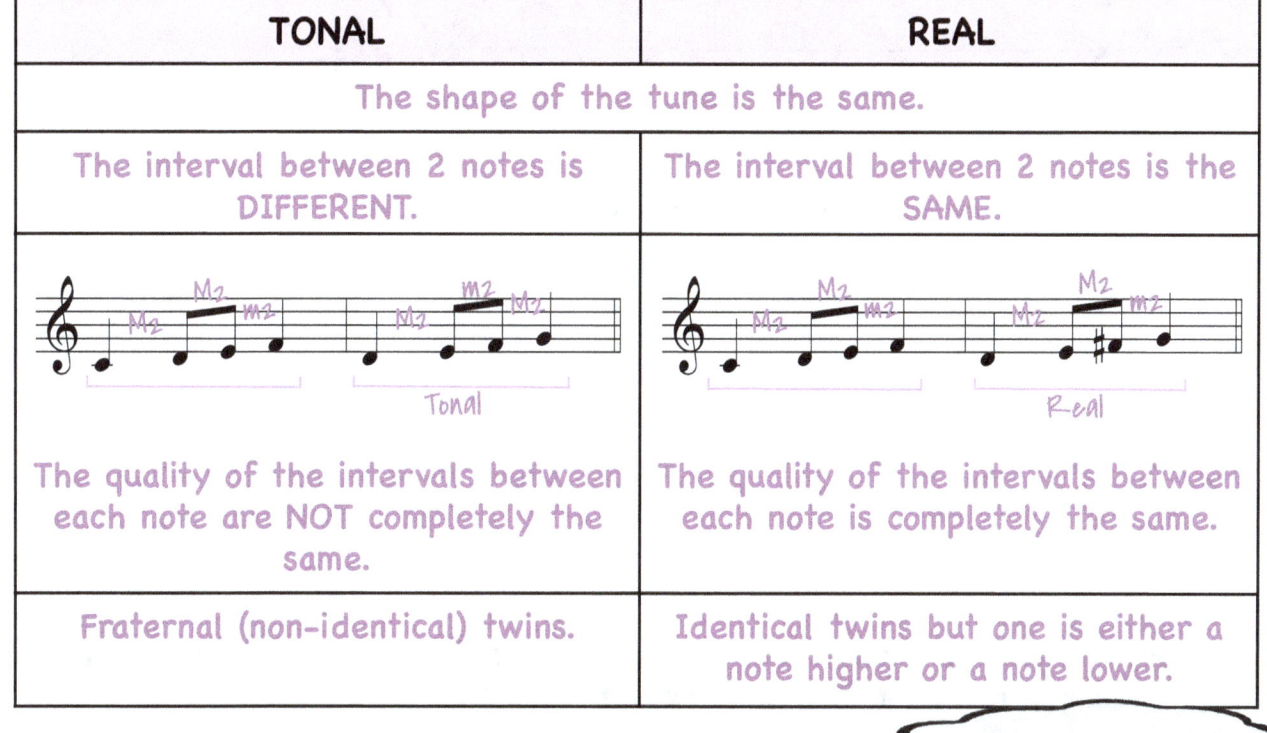

Write a bracket to show the sequences and label them as 'tonal' or 'real'.

4-Part Vocal Style

4-Part Vocal Style is usually known in a choir as SATB - Soprano, Alto, Tenor, and Bass. This is where each part sits on the grand stave.

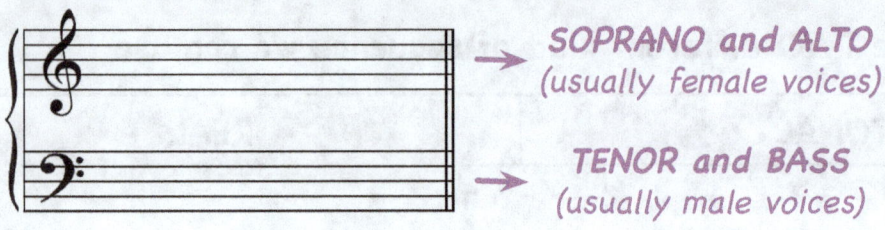

SOPRANO and ALTO
(usually female voices)

TENOR and BASS
(usually male voices)

Below shows the common voice range for each part.

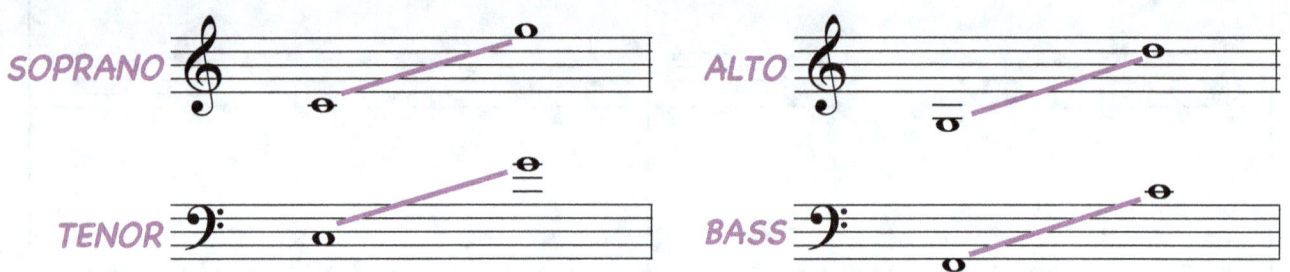

In 4-Part Vocal Style, there are different rules for stem directions as shown in the example below on the tonic key of A minor.

If the stem is facing upwards, it means the higher voices read the top line.

If the stem is facing downwards, it means that the lower voices read the lower line.

When we write a 4-part vocal style, each part uses a different note from a chord but we double the root note to cover the fourth part.
For example, these are the notes we use in C major.

C E G C

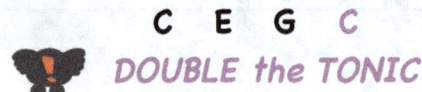 DOUBLE the TONIC

1. Write out the notes of the tonic triads of these keys.

   A minor   A C E A   G major   _____   B minor   _____

   D major   _____   E minor   _____   C major   _____

   F major   _____   B♭ major _____   D minor   _____

When writing 4-Part Vocal Style, each part needs to be a certain distance between each other.

SOPRANO
↕ *within one octave*
ALTO
↕ *within one octave*
TENOR
↕ *within two octave*
BASS

NO overlapping of parts.

The bass ALWAYS sings the root note.

2. Below are chords in 4-Part Vocal Style written in the key of C major. Cross out the bar that is incorrectly written.

3. Circle the TWO roots in the following chords.

47

4. Label the triads in exercise No. 3 using Roman Numerals.

Unison intervals are a possibility but only between the tenor and the bass part. Below are how they would look in semibreves and notes with stems in the tonic key of G major.

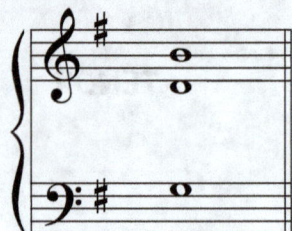

Draw the root note TWICE when you are writing the tenor and bass part in unison.

5. Using crotchet notes, write in 4-Part Vocal Style using the tonic chords shown by the Roman Numerals.

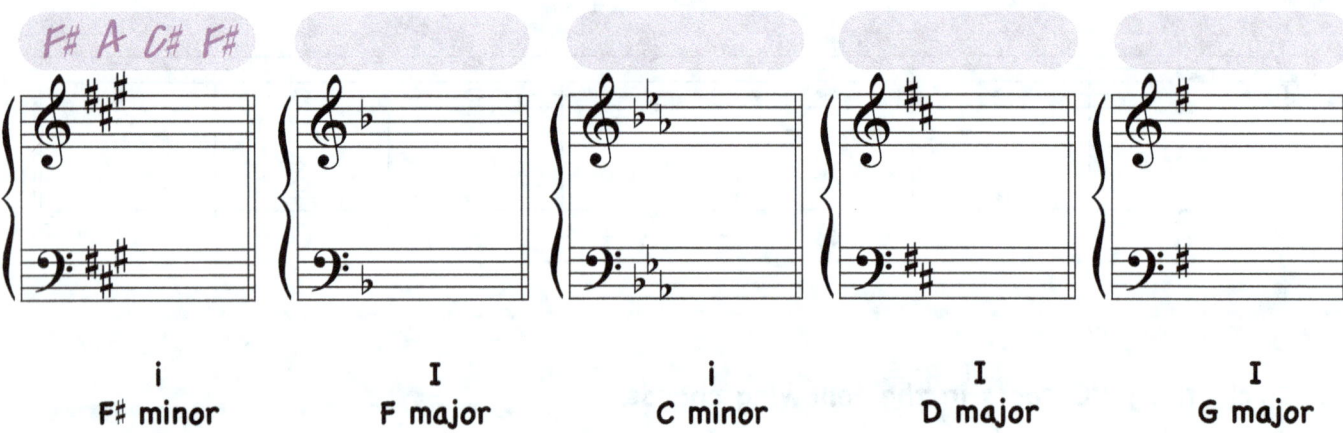

F# A C# F#

i — F# minor
I — F major
i — C minor
I — D major
I — G major

6. Using minim notes, write in 4-Part Vocal Style using the chords shown by the Roman Numerals.

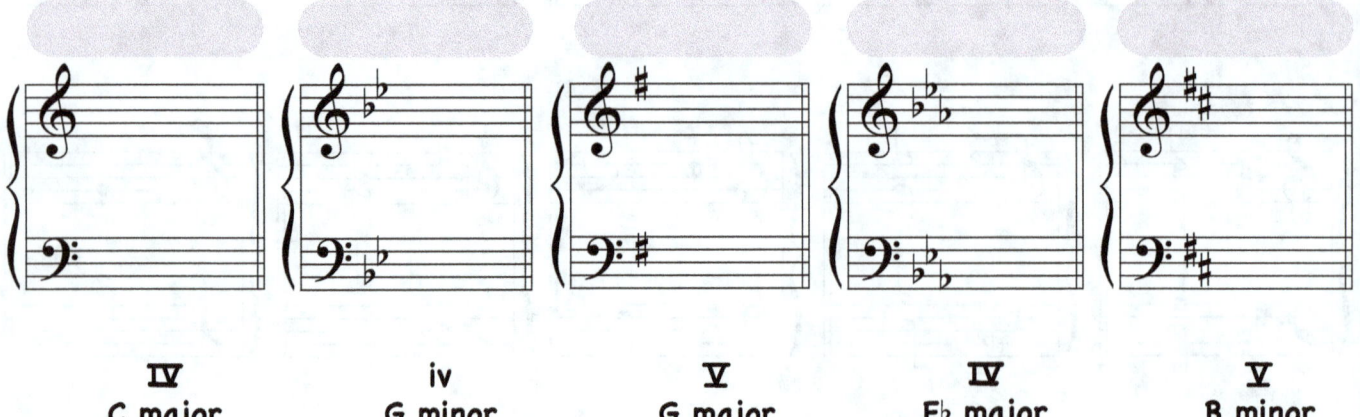

IV — C major
iv — G minor
V — G major
IV — E♭ major
V — B minor

48

Cadences

A cadence is a chord progression of at least TWO chords that ends a musical phrase.

There are 4 different types of cadences.

CADENCE
- Perfect
- Imperfect
- Plagal
- Interrupted

In Grade 3, we will only be looking into the 2 main cadences which are the Perfect and Plagal cadence.

PERFECT	PLAGAL
Completes the phrase (sentence)	
Ends on tonic note	
Full close	
Strong, definite ending – "THE END!!" sounding	Gentler ending – "A-men" sounding which is used in hymns
Uses the dominant and tonic triad	Uses the subdominant and tonic triad
V – I / i	IV – I
Eg. (F major)	Eg. (F major)
V I	IV I

Steps – Draw...
1. the letter notes of the triad
2. notes for the bass part
   (ALWAYS a root note)
3. note in common
   (On any one part only)
4. leading note moving to the tonic
   (On any one part only)
5. left over notes
   (On any one part only)
	Steps – Draw...
	1. the letter notes of the triad
	2. notes for the bass part
	   (ALWAYS a root note)
	3. note in common
	   (On any one part only)
	4. left over notes
	   (Moving by step)

1. Which TWO chords represent the Perfect cadence?

2. Which TWO chords represent the Plagal cadence?

3. Which note should the bass part always be in?

4. Using minim notes, write perfect cadences in these major keys.

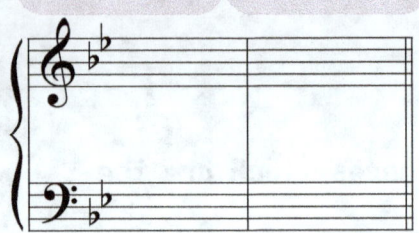 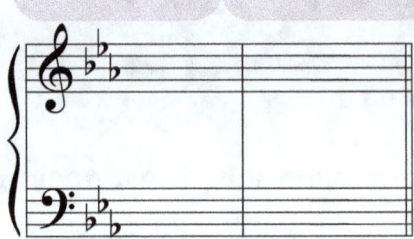 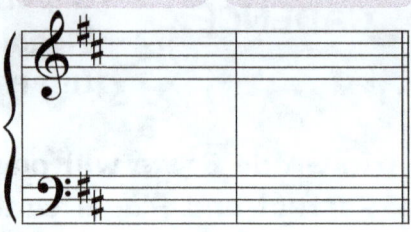

5. Using minim notes, write perfect cadences in these minor keys.
   Raise the leading note to change the dominant into a major triad.

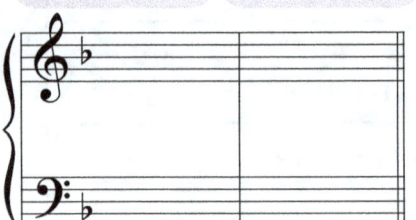 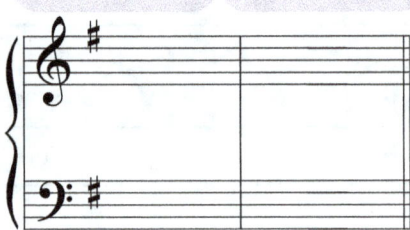 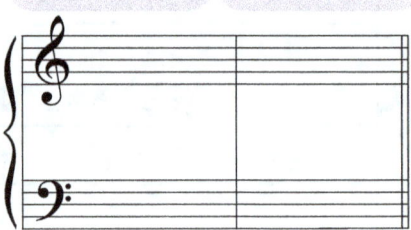

6. Using minim notes, write plagal cadences in these major keys.

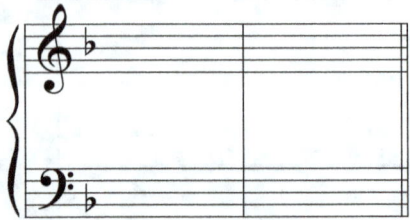 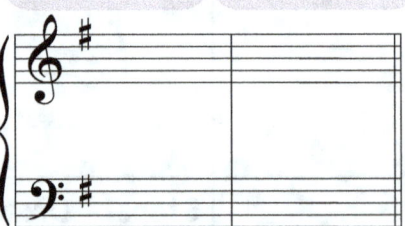 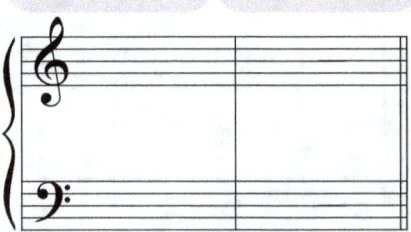

7. Using minim notes, write plagal cadences in these minor keys.

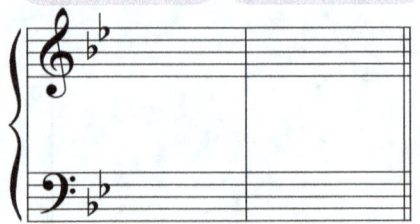  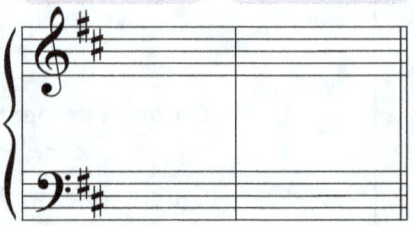

8. Label all the cadences in exercise No. 4 to 7 using Roman Numerals.

9. Name each key and its cadence as either perfect or plagal.

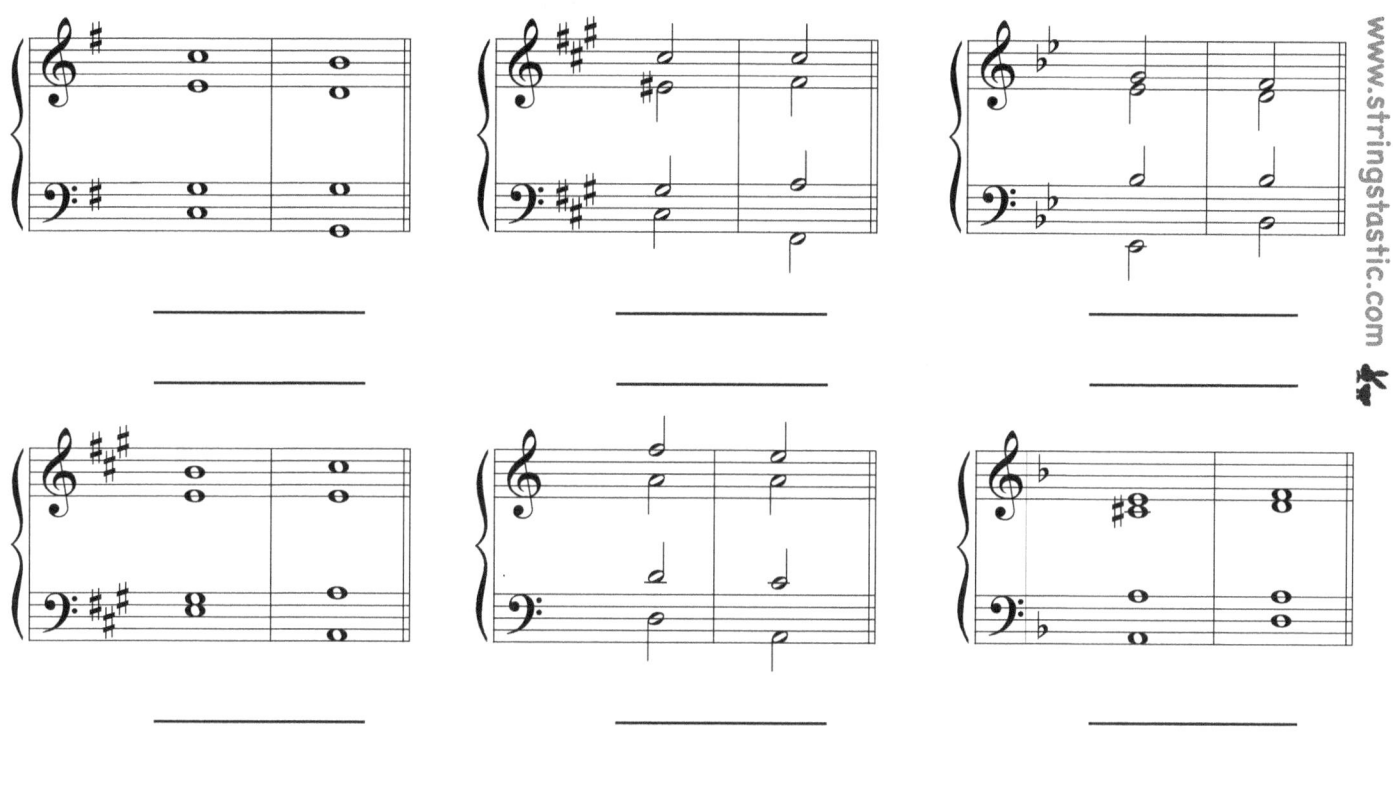

10. Using minim notes, write out the key signature and following cadences.

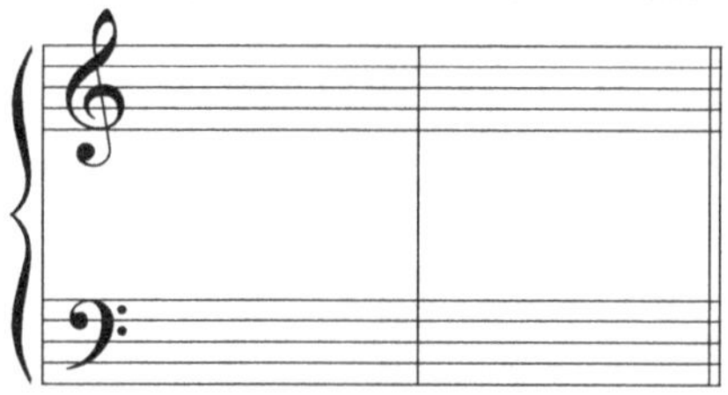

| D minor | A major | A major |
| Plagal | Plagal | Perfect |

| E♭ major | G minor | E major |
| Plagal | Perfect | Plagal |

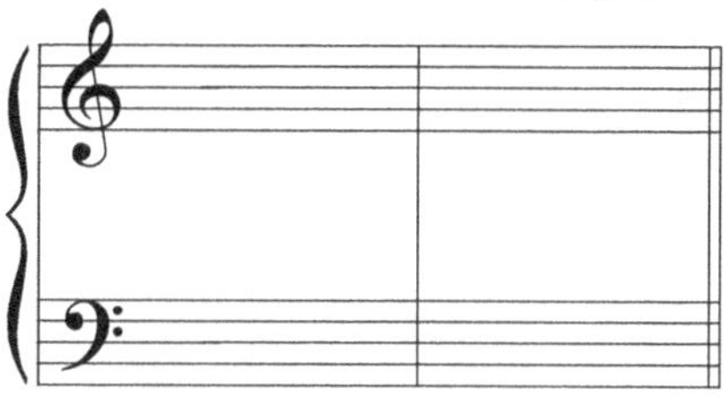

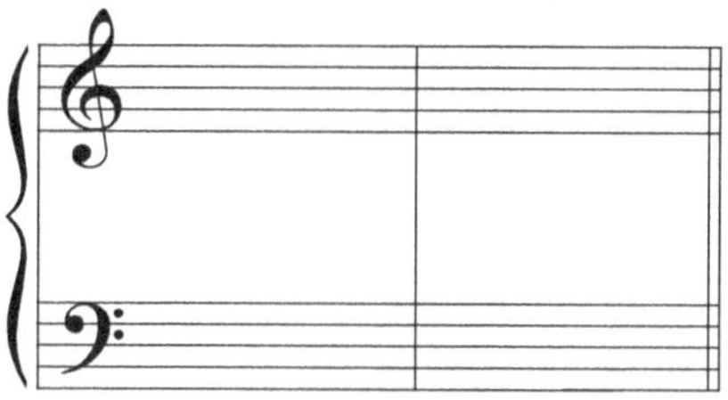

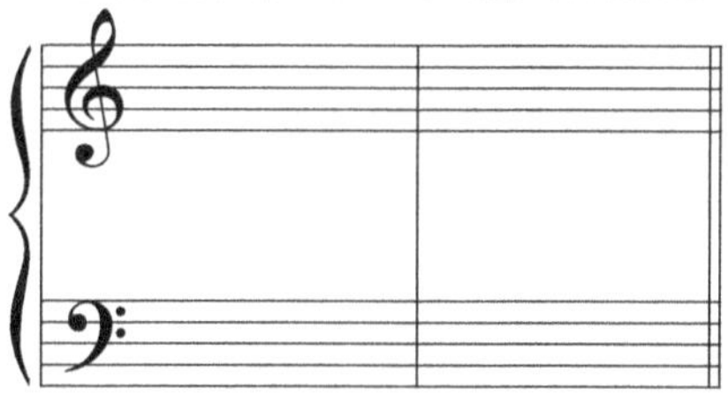

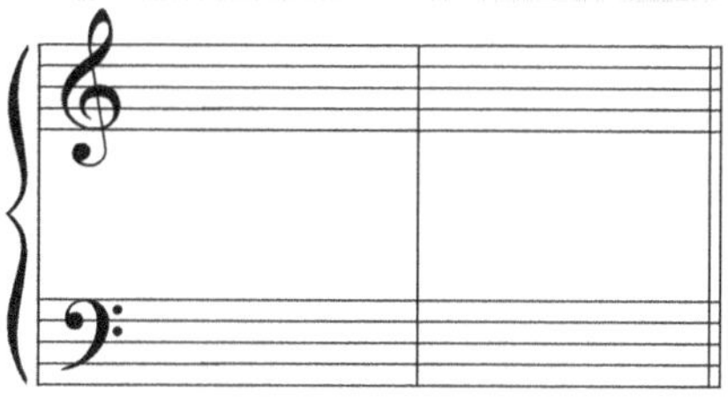

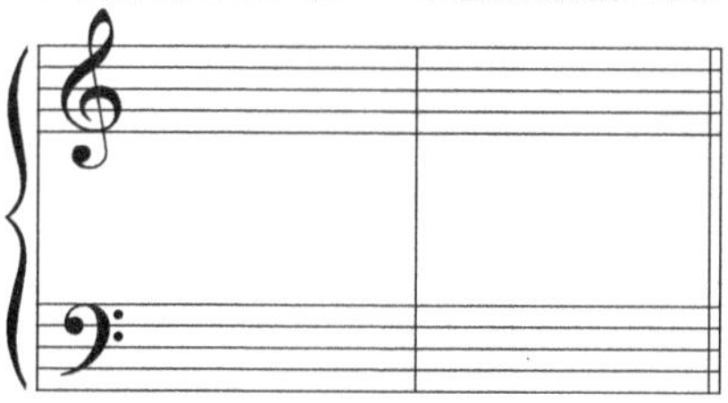

51

Revision

1. Draw these notes at the same pitch on the alto clef.

2. Write the scale of F♯ melodic minor on the treble clef
   - Use key signature
   - One octave in an ascending and descending order
   - Use quaver notes grouped in pairs
   - Mark each semitone with a slur
   - Complete the scale with a double bar line

3. Write a suitable rhythmic pattern to the following couplet.

   Roar loudly at our little house

   And shake the window sills!

4. Name these scales and in semibreves, write out the primary triads.

5. Label the primary triads in exercise No. 3 using Roman Numerals and chord symbols.

52

6. In minims, use the appropriate key signature and triads accordingly for each of the following keys.

G minor	A major	E♭ major	B minor
Tonic	Subdominant	Dominant	Dominant
Root position	2nd inversion	Root position	1st inversion

7. Use a single root note of each triad shown by the chord symbols to write the bass line.

8. Label each bar with the appropriate Roman Numeral and write a tune using notes from the tonic or dominant triads shown below.

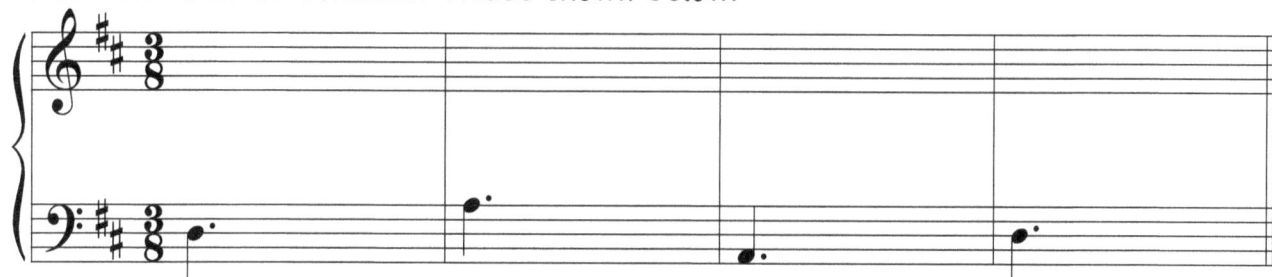

9. Write a bracket to show the sequence and label it as 'tonal' or 'real'.

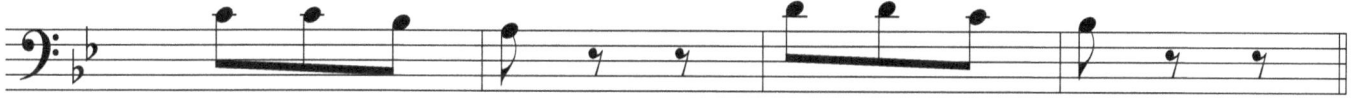

10. Using crotchet notes in a 4-Part Vocal Style, write out the key signature and following cadences.

D major	B♭ major	F♯ minor
Plagal	Perfect	Perfect

Transposition

Music transposition refers to moving a collection of notes up or down into a different key or clef to suit a player's music range or to make it easier for the player to read the notes.

In Grade 3, we will only learn to transpose into different keys and between clefs. You will come across all sorts of accidentals which you would have to include. But be careful as sometimes these accidentals change depending on the key.

1. Transposing in the same key but different clefs.

For example, below is a tune in C major.

Here is how the tune looks like when transposed an octave lower into the bass clef.

Use the following method to help you transpose.
- Draw out the new clef and adjust the position of the key signature accordingly
- Write out the time signature
- Name the first note of the tune given
- Find and draw the note on the new clef
- Write out the tune with the same intervals between the notes (Follow the note movement of the melody)
- Draw in any accidentals where needed
- Check that the last note of the tune is the same letter name as the orignal tune.

For Grade 3, alto clef is not required. However, for the curious mind, here is how you transpose a tune into the alto clef.

Use the rules listed above. The only difference is that the middle C on the alto clef is as shown on the right.

Middle C

Here is how the tune looks when transposed into the alto clef.

1. **Transpose these tunes down an octave into the bass clef.**

 Draw the clef, key signature and double bar lines.

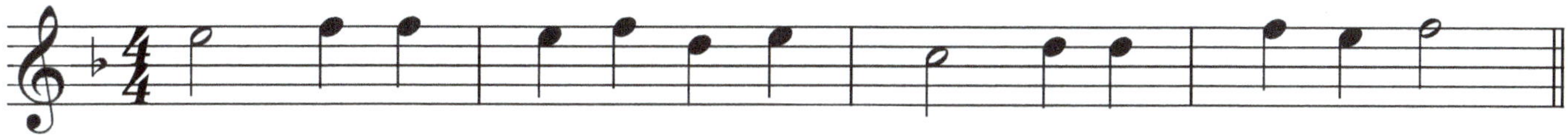

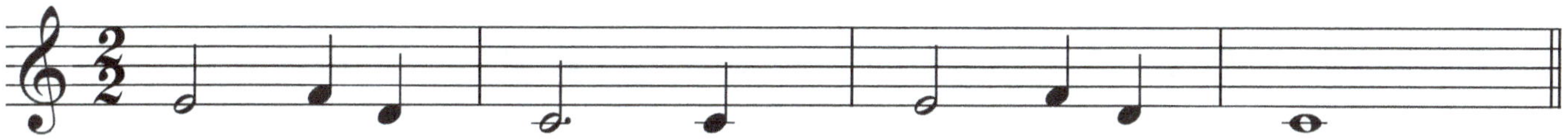

2. **Transpose all the three tunes in exercise No.1 into the alto clef.**

 Take note that the position of the notes and key signature would be different.

 See if you can play these short tunes in exercise No.1 and 2 by reading them on different clefs. Was it easy?

3. Transpose these tunes up an octave into the treble clef.

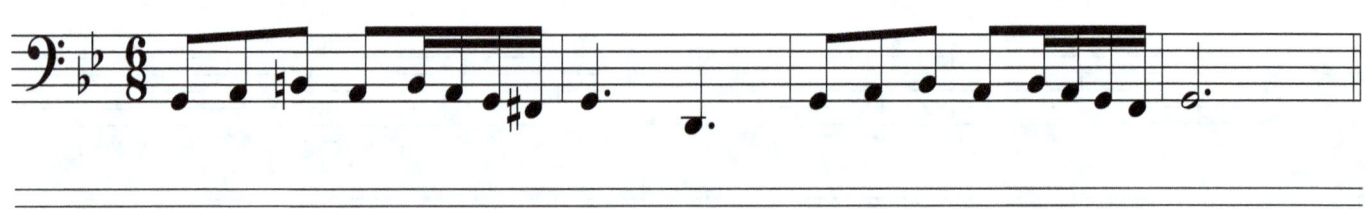

2. Transposing to a different key.

 Use the same rules on the previous page. The only difference is that the note names will be different.

Here are the steps on transposing a tune to D major.

1. Key signature of original key - C
2. Name of the first note - C
3. New key - D major
4. Starting note of the new key - D
5. Distance from C major to D major - 1 step up
(the whole tune moves up by 1 step)

Here is how the tune looks. Notice how the accidentals remain the same.

Here is how the tune looks when transposed to B♭ major.

⚠️ The accidentals change because of the new key. Notice how the note is still rising or falling accordingly.

4. Transpose these tunes to D minor in the same clef.

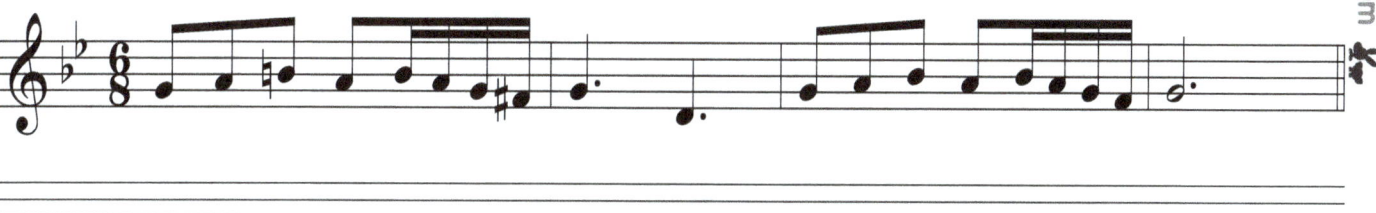

5. Transpose these tunes to E major in the same clef.

See if you can play these short tunes in exercise No.4 and 5 by reading them on different clefs and keys. Was it easy?

Similar Motion VS. Contrary Motion

SIMILAR MOTION	CONTRARY MOTION
Two or more parts move in the same direction (Parallel direction)	Two or more parts move in the opposite direction

Parts moving in similar or contrary motion can be written between the same or different clefs.

Below is an example of TWO parts moving in Similar Motion (moving in the same direction).

1. In which direction do parts moving in similar motion go? _____

2. In which direction do parts moving in contrary motion go? _____

3. Write TWO more repeats of these bars to make ostinati that move in similar motion.

Below is an example of TWO parts moving in Contrary Motion (moving in the opposite direction),

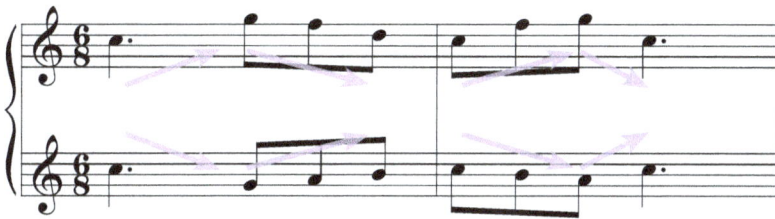

4. Write **TWO** more repeats of these bars to make ostinati that move in contrary motion.

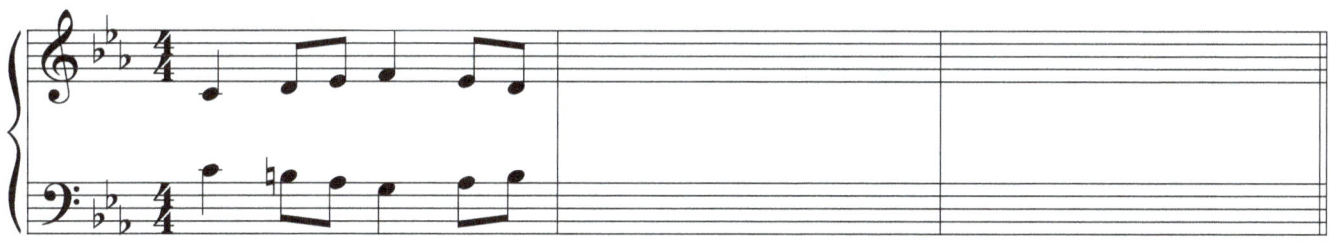

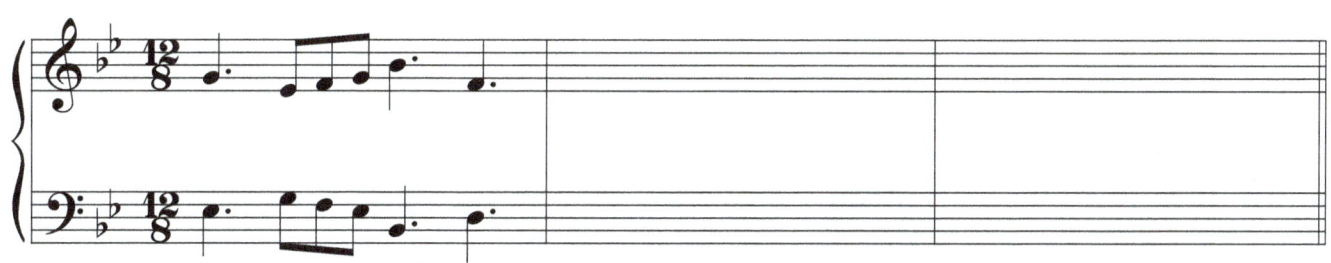

Let us play the parts in exercise No. 3 and 4 together with another player to hear how it sounds.

Musical Words and Symbols

Tempo is the speed at which music is played. It is usually placed ABOVE the music at the beginning of a piece.

1. Let us revise what we have learnt in Grades 1 and 2. Fill in the blanks where needed.

   Prestissimo - extremely fast
   Vivace or **Vivo -** _____
   Allegro - _____
   Allegretto - _____
   Moderato - _____
   Andante - _____
   Adagio or **Lento -** _____

   mosso or **moto -** _____
   meno - _____
   piu - _____
   con moto - with movement
   animato or **animando -** animated
   agitato - agitated
   Ad libitum - at pleasure, quite freely
   rubato - rhythmic freedom
   (Performer does not stick strictly to the time to give more expression to the performance.)

2. Write the tempo markings you have learnt on this short tunes. Then, circle the anacrusis of each tune.

It's a world of laugh-ter, a world of tears.

Expression Markings
Expression Marking tells a player in what kind of mood to play the music. They are written below the music.

anima - feeling
brio - spirit
forza - force
grazioso - _____
giocoso - playful, merry
tranquillo - calmly

forte-piano (fp) - loud then immediately soft
sforzando (sfz) - strong accent
calando - getting softer and slower
leggiero - lightly
marziale - march-like
morendo - dying away

Other Markings

al, alla - like
con - with
largamente - broadly
larghetto - rather broadly
loco - normal pitch
opus (Op.) - a work or group of works

As a string player, although we do not need to know the terms below as they are meant for piano players, these would be helpful to know.

Una corda (U.C) - with soft pedal
Tre corde (T.C) - release soft pedal
Main droite (M.D) - right hand
Main gauche (M.G) - left hand
R.H. - right hand
L.H. - left hand

> Sometimes the way we remember meanings or terms is by looking at the first few letters of the music term. It is usually close to the english definition.

Articulation
Articulation refers to symbols used on notes to create different sounds.

3. Fill in the blanks to the articulation markings in terms of how we play them as a string player.

Articulation	Description
Staccato	Short, sharp and detached
Accent	
Marcato	Marked, accented (Louder version of an accent.)
Tenuto	Slightly lengthen and sustained (Hold for full value of the note.)
Slur	
Semi-staccato	Hook notes (Same bow direction. Half staccato - halfway between a slur and staccato.)

Let us revise where music words and terminologies should be written on the stave.

(Tempo Markings)

(Dynamics or Expression Markings)

Final Revision

1. Name these scales and in semibreves, write out the primary triads.

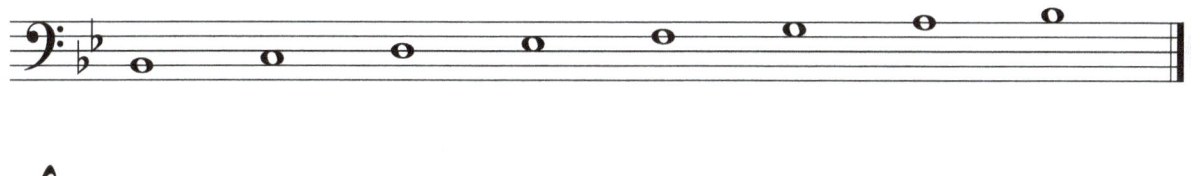

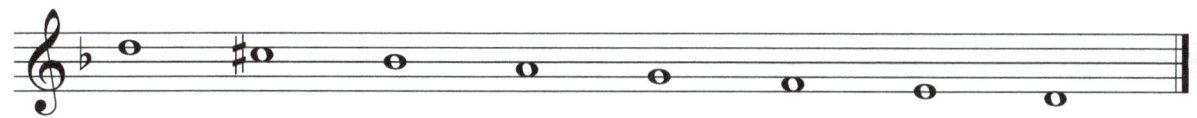

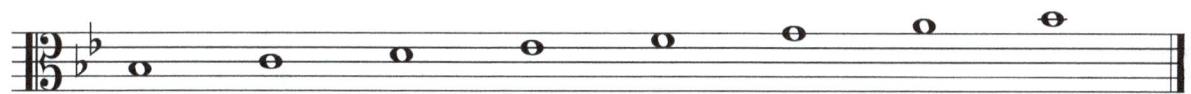

2. Label the primary triads in exercise No. 1 using Roman Numerals and chord symbols.

3. Without looking back on your notes, write out the correct technical names for these scale degree.

1	2	3	4	5	6	7
Tonic						

4. Name these scale degree.

Key	Note	Scale Degree Name
G minor	A	
B♭ major	E♭	
E♭ major	E♭	
C minor	G	
A major	G♯	

5. Circle the correct answer. The sequence below is   REAL / TONAL .

6. Answer the questions in each square.

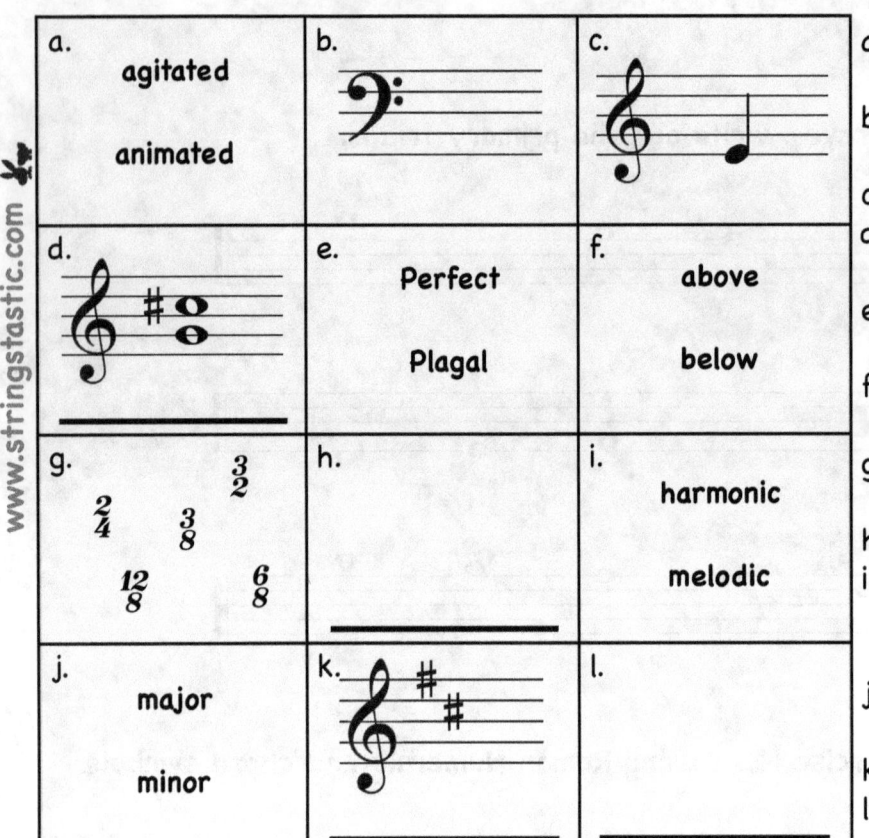

a. Circle the correct definition for *animato*.
b. Draw the key signature of E major.
c. Place a marcato sign on the note.
d. Name the interval and its quality.
e. Which cadence do these two chords represent? IV - I
f. Dynamic markings are written _____ the stave.
g. Circle the time signature which represents a compound time.
h. Draw triplet notes and label them.
i. A _____ interval is when the notes are drawn on top of each other.
j. In a minor key, the dominant triad is always a _____ chord.
k. Name the minor key.
l. Draw a sforzando symbol.

7. In semibreves, use the appropriate key signature and triads accordingly for each of the following keys.

E minor	C major	A major	G minor
Dominant	Dominant	Tonic	Subdominant
Semibreve	Quaver	Minim	Crotchet
Root position	1st inversion	2nd inversion	1st inversion

8. Write a suitable rhythmic pattern to the following couplet.

Easter time at last is here,

Bunnies, chickies, let us cheer.

9. Label each bar with the appropriate Roman Numeral and write a tune using notes from the tonic or dominant triads shown below.

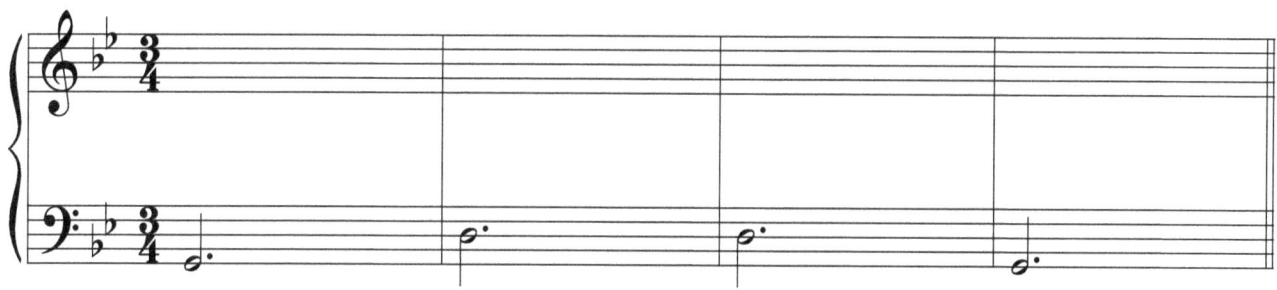

10. Using minim notes in a 4-Part Vocal Style, write out the key signature and following cadences.

D major
Plagal

E♭ major
Perfect

C♯ minor
Perfect

11. Write TWO more repeats of this ostinati.

12. Make a sequence by repeating this bar twice, one note lower each time using the given tune.

13. Circle the correct answer. The sequence shown in exercises No. 9 and 10 is moving in SIMILAR / CONTRARY motion.

Analysis

1. Look at the following piece and answer the questions below. Only some of the answers are given.

Martin J. Nystrom

a. Which major key is this piece in? _____

b. What note is the tonic in this piece? _____

c. What note is sol in this piece? _____

d. What are the rests in bar 2 and bar 4 called? _____

e. Write a Roman Numeral below the last chord of this piece to show that the tonic chord accompanies the tune.

f. Write a Roman Numeral below the last crotchet beat of bar 14 to show that the subdominant chord accompanies the tune.

g. Which phrase ends with a IV-I chord progression? _____

h. What cadence does this piece end with? _____

i. Name the interval between the tenor and bass parts marked with astericks (*) in bar 2.
_____

j. What does ♩ = 70 mean? _____

k. How many phrases does this piece have? _____

l. How many tied notes are there in this piece? _____

m. Is this piece in a simple or compound time? _____

n. What is the time signature of this piece? _____

o. What is the scale degree of the treble clef note in bar 12? _____

p. What are these notes, ♫ in bar 4 called and how do you play them? _____
_____

q. Describe the dynamic markings in this piece. _____
_____

r. Does this piece start on an up-beat or a down-beat? _____

s. What is the musical word for music that does not start on the first beat of the bar?
_____

67

Pretty As A Picture

Mark Matthews
(Australian Composer)

If you are interested to look at more of Mark's music, please visit, www.remarkablemusic.net .

a. Which major key is this piece in? _____

b. What note is the tonic in this piece? _____

c. What note is sol in this piece? _____

d. Write a chord symbol above the last chord of this piece to show that the tonic chord accompanies the tune.

e. Write a chord symbol above the second last bar to show that the dominant chord accompanies the tune.

f. What cadence does this piece end with? _____

g. Which part plays the main tune in this piece? _____

h. Name the interval between the two notes marked with astericks (*) in bar 11.
   _____

i. What does $\quarternote = 65$ mean? _____

j. Using letter names, name the last note of the piece on the treble clef. _____

k. Using letter names, name the last note of the piece on the bass clef. _____

l. Is this piece in a simple or compound time? _____

m. What is the time signature of this piece? _____

n. What is the scale degree of the treble clef note in bar 12? _____

o. What are these notes, $\overset{3}{\eighthnotetriplet}$ in bar 4 called and how do you play them? _____
   _____

p. Describe the dynamic markings in this piece. _____
   _____

q. Does this piece start on an up-beat or a down-beat? _____

r. What does ritardando mean? _____

s. How would you describe the shape of the bass clef? _____
   _____

At the Day's End

Adagio ♩=72
Calmly

Margaret Brandman
(Australian Composer)

'Used by Permission' from Margaret Brandman. If you are interested to look at more of Margaret's music, please visit, www.margaretbrandmanmusic.com .

a. Which major key is this piece in? _____

b. What note is the tonic in this piece? _____

c. What note is fa in this piece? _____

d. Write a chord symbol above the last chord of this piece to show that the tonic chord accompanies the tune.

e. Write a chord symbol above the last minim note of the second last bar to show that the dominant chord accompanies the tune.

f. What cadence does this piece end with? _____

g. What does 𝒫𝑒𝑑. on the last bar of the piece mean? _____

h. Name the interval between the two notes marked with astericks (*) in bar 5.
   _____

i. What does ♩ = 72 mean? _____

j. Using letter names, in bar 16, name the last note of the bass clef. _____

k. On the last bar, what does R.H. mean? _____

l. Is this piece in a simple or compound time? _____

m. What is the time signature of this piece? _____

n. What is the scale degree of the treble clef note in bar 12? _____

o. What do the numbers on top or next to the note represent? _____
   _____

p. Describe the dynamic markings in this piece. _____
   _____

q. Does this piece start on an up-beat or a down-beat? _____

r. What does rit. mean? _____

q. Describe the rhythmic patern of the treble clef in the first TWO bars of each line?
   _____
   _____

71